Foreword

"Hitch your wagon to a star."
—Ralph Waldo Emerson

If you want to become known on the job as a self-starter or maintain the habit of easily self-starting, this book is for you. Jeff Davidson has structured *The 60 Second Self-Starter* so that each of the sixty tips, one tip for each minute in an hour, can be absorbed in about a minute or less.

Jeff and I both feel that this book should be employed as an active resource. When you find yourself at an impasse at work, flip through its pages and find three or four tips that appear helpful.

If you're that rare person who is committed to taking proactive steps to stay productive, you might be more inclined to read the book sequentially. To derive its full benefits, however, keep this book nearby and flip through it quickly to get yourself up and going whenever you encounter roadblocks.

Jeff has arranged *The 60 Second Self-Starter* into six major sections: *Adopt the Right Mindset, Set Yourself Up to Win, Give Yourself the Edge, Come Out Charging, Take on the Harder Tasks,* and *Soar to Great Heights*. This sequence will carry you through in the face of tasks and projects large and small. It's your option to proceed sequentially or not. One single tip, or two, or three, often will enable you to dislodge your current barriers.

The sixty tips range from time-tested techniques to fresh and innovative insights that career professionals and people in general have found to be helpful. As he has done with so many others before, Jeff has written this book in an engaging, friendly, witty, down-to-earth style. You'll feel as if he is conversing with you as a friend, not preaching to you.

Throughout, he shares with you the insider techniques and vital lessons he has learned over the years that helped him become a self-starter par excellence. Whether you are stalled on the smallest of tasks, or on major projects with long time spans, you'll find that *The 60 Second Self-Starter* is both a valuable tool and an action guide for helping you become more accomplished and more satisfied with your work and your life. As such, I believe that you will find great value in this book.

—Mac Anderson, Founder
Successories
Aurora, Illinois

60 SECOND
SELF-STARTER

Sixty Solid Techniques for Motivating Yourself at Work

JEFF DAVIDSON

BUSINESS

avon, massach

Published by Adams Business
Adams Media, an F+W Publications Company
57 Littlefield Street, Avon, MA 02322. U.S.A.
www.adamsmedia.com

This book is a revised edition of
The 60 Second Procrastinator by Jeff Davidson,
copyright © 2003 by F+W Publications, Inc.,
ISBN 10: 1-58062-923-7, ISBN 13: 978-1-58062-923-2.

ISBN-10: 1-59869-843-5
ISBN-13: 978-1-59869-843-5

Printed in the United States of America.

J I H G F E D C B A

Library of Congress Cataloging-in-Publication Data
is available from the publisher.

This publication is designed to provide accurate and authoritative information with
regard to the subject matter covered. It is sold with the understanding that the publisher is not engaged in rendering legal, accounting, or other professional advice. If
legal advice or other expert assistance is required, the services of a competent professional person should be sought.
  —From a *Declaration of Principles* jointly adopted by a Committee of the
American Bar Association and a Committee of Publishers and Associations

Many of the designations used by manufacturers and sellers to distinguish their
product are claimed as trademarks. Where those designations appear in this book
and Adams Media was aware of a trademark claim, the designations have been
printed with initial capital letters.

*This book is available at quantity discounts for bulk purchases.
For information, please call 1-800-289-0963.*

Contents

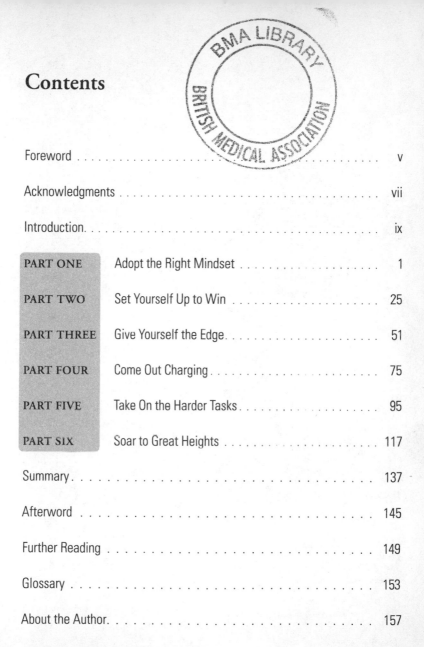

Acknowledgments

Jessica Scism, Liz Ward, Cat Hickey, and Brian Willett helped me in the preparation of this book by making key edits and revisions. Peter Archer, my editor, offered enthusiasm for the revised project and made it a "go" along with Laura Daly, editorial director. My thanks goes to Beth Gissinger in Publicity and Promotions, Karen Cooper and Phil Sexton in Marketing and Sales, and Chris Duffy in International Rights and Distribution. My thanks also to Scott Watrous for keeping company operations in the past on an even keel and to Bob Adams for his constant vision and excellence.

A number of subject matter experts also need to be cited, including Dr. Piers Steel, Alan Lakein, Robert Fritz, Dennis Hensley, Lynn Lively, Frieda Porat, Dr. William Knaus, Edwin Bliss, Daniel Goleman, Dean Smith, Robert Fulghum, William Osler, David Viscott, M.D., Betty Friedan, Wayne Dyer, John Grisham, Jim Cathcart, Shad Helmstetter, Dwight Stones, Susan Jeffers, Aubrey Daniels, Roger Dawson, Maxwell Maltz, Alyce Cornyn Selby, Julia Cameron, Debra Benton, Dr. William Maples, and Joe Sugarman, for their ideas, influence, support, or contributions to specific tips.

Introduction

Is the following list at all reminiscent of you?

- You find yourself having a hard time getting started on tasks that you know are important.
- You spend oodles of time on dreadfully menial tasks.
- You're late filing your taxes (knowing that gazillions of others are doing so as well is not an excuse).
- You hold on to the same lackluster job because it is familiar.
- You avoid making out a will because you don't want to contemplate your own mortality.
- You send greeting cards from the Hallmark "belated" selection.
- You shop for Christmas presents on December 24.
- You schedule a health checkup months after suspecting that something is wrong.
- You have drawers in your desk, files in your cabinet, whole closets, or whole rooms that are total disaster areas— you've been "meaning to organize them" for a long time.
- You actually begin some projects after the deadline because you need that kind of anxiety to set you in motion.

The Free Dictionary defines the term *self-starter* as "One who displays an unusual amount of initiative." Displaying great initiative in today's ultracompetitive work environment is certainly desirable if you want to rapidly advance in your career. On your path to becoming a self-starter, however, or maintaining your self-starter reputation, you may need to overcome an undesirable behavior you've picked up along the way. Yessiree, I'm referring to procrastination, which has been described as the act of putting off something until a later time, either by not starting a task or by not finishing one you've started.

The basic definition of procrastination, however, doesn't encompass the wide range of emotions that people associate with the term. Individuals who procrastinate may regard themselves as unproductive and lazy, and that's just the printable version. They report feeling anxious, ineffectual, guilty, or immobile.

Procrastination: The Antithesis of Self-Starting Behavior

An insidious result occurs when you allow procrastination to diminish your experience of the present. For example, you bring work home over the weekend, but you never look at it. Meanwhile, knowing you intended to handle it, you decline to participate in leisure activities that would have actually contributed to a better frame of mind. As Shakespeare might have said, "Measure for measure, you want to treasure your leisure."

Procrastinators tend to be people with a low tolerance for frustration—a scholarly way of saying that they give up too easily and too soon. They also tend to be perfectionists, with a high need for autonomy and approval. Capping off the profile, they have a high fear of failure. So . . . some poor souls procrastinate because the tasks or projects before them represent high stakes, which they approach with dread. Then they rationalize the situation by saying, "Who wants to get started anyway?" Do *you* know anyone remotely like that?

If you're a procrastinator, you're not alone. It's estimated that procrastinators account for 15 to 20 percent of the population.

Not sure if you're a procrastinator or not? Well, if you're into math . . . now there's a formula to help you figure it out.

Dr. Piers Steel, a University of Calgary professor in the Haskayne School of Business, has developed an equation to predict procrastination. Steel rejects traditional assumptions about the source of procrastination. Many people think that perfectionism is at the root of procrastination, but he asserts that low self-confidence prevents individuals from approaching tasks that they fear they might not be able to complete. Steel also cites other contributing factors such as how distractible or impulsive a person might be, as well as how averse one is to a particular task. Impulsive behaviors and temptations can be so difficult to resist. This is why we check our e-mail several times instead of completing a project, and why we eat a lot of bread at a restaurant before the meal is served.

Dr. Steel fortunately notes, however, that willpower is a powerful force. Steel's Temporal Motivational Theory takes into account the expectation of success (E), the value of completion (V), the immediacy (I) and the individual's sensitivity to delay (D) in order to calculate the task's desirability or utility (U). Got all that? So here's the formula to predict the likelihood of procrastination:

$$A \text{ Task's Desirability or Utility} = E \times V / I \times D.$$

Would you rather skip the math stuff? Me too! Here's the skinny: To break the procrastination habit, "The old saying is true," Dr. Steel concludes. "Whether you believe you can or believe you can't, you're probably right." So identify what obstacles could potentially interfere with your success, and plan ahead for them. Simply accomplishing one goal—achieving a small win—can give you the resolve to tackle others, making you more confident in your ability to succeed.

Dyed-in-the-wool?

Even if you're a dyed-in-the-wool procrastinator, undoubtedly (we hope) there are some areas of your life in which you probably shine. After all, nobody drags their feet all the time, and all of us have areas in our lives in which we display a nice touch of self-starting. In any event, *never let bouts of procrastination diminish your self-worth or self-esteem.* You're still a good person, and your mother probably loves you. If you've had birth, then you have worth.

The inability to get started affects business executives, entrepreneurs, homemakers, retirees, students, and everyone in between. William Knaus, a psychologist, estimated that 90 percent of college students procrastinate. Of these students, about 25 percent are chronic procrastinators, and Knaus observes that they are usually the students who end up dropping out of college and probably end up running major software companies and owning 2.8 billion shares of the company's stock.

Perhaps the single greatest impediment to getting things done, at least among students, but increasingly among career professionals, is instant messaging (IM). Whereas e-mail or Facebook messages can take up to a few minutes to arrive in your inbox, as you know, IMs pop up instantaneously, kind of like creepy ghosts in a fun house. Many students and professionals become addicted to IM.

There you are, moving along nicely on something when, bingo, faster than you can say "significant other," an IM pops up on your screen. It doesn't matter what program you are using or what else you're working on. While text messages can be avoided by shutting off your phone, an IM flashes reminders on the screen, like an itch waiting to be scratched.

Some people feel as if they are isolated from the world when they are not signed on to IM, going so far as to keep it running (even if only to display their "away message") while they are studying or in class and—unbelievably to the over-thirty set—during final exams. We have enough youth; how about a fountain of smart?

This marvel of the information age raises a plaguing question: Will attention spans, concentration, and focus ever return to what they used to be? Will we be pulled in so many different directions that the ability to stick to a single task will become obsolete? Of course, one could argue that if you are unfocused and have a high proclivity to procrastinate, the means at your disposal are immaterial. Instant Messenger is but one of a long line of vehicles that procrastinators have employed. In the rice bowl of life it is not even a grain. In the near future there will be other, even more enticing distractions such as highly interactive, conversant imaginary friends—avatars—not to mention virtual reality opportunities that will make you never want to come back to this world.

Distractions abound in today's workplace. It is not so easy to work in an office where all the desks are placed in one open space. Alternatively, the widespread installation of cubicles in some offices also contributes to the noise and confusion that permeates the workplace and has made Scott Adams (Dilbert, Dogbert, Catbert) a rich man. Working all day in an environment that is rife with noisy distractions from coworkers does little to help the individual whose powers of concentration are already strained. The sad reality of too many office environments today is that they actually contribute to procrastination and a decline in productivity.

I know of people who go to extraordinary lengths to mask their procrastination, sometimes concocting stories—whoppers, really—and sometimes creating scenarios that divert attention. Some steal hours from their employers by engaging in endless Web surfing or finding numerous offline diversions. Procrastination has been known to contribute to absenteeism and tardiness.

Above All, a Nasty Habit

Procrastination is a habit that has affected people since they were cave dwellers wearing animal skins, and wild poodles roamed the earth. Whatever task or project needs to be completed, whether it's at work or even at home, a person today potentially faces more distractions than at any other time in history. Procrastination is facilitated by distraction!

Whenever you let progress on lower-level tasks or projects stand in the way of higher-level tasks or projects, you are procrastinating—you got that? (Note: To keep the terminology in this book simple, I'll use *task* or *project* to mean some single, near-term job, objective, or desired end result. *Goals* will mean specific actions, objectives, or strategies to execute tasks or projects in support of priorities. *Priorities* are the things that are most important to you, the pinnacle being life priorities. Now repeat that back to me. . . .) Procrastination, when viewed from a cultural standpoint, is a response to all that is competing for your attention. It is actually harder to be a self-starter now than at any other time in history because there are more ways to go astray. To quote from my favorite author:

> *"When* everyone *is too busy, don't expect a more productive society, expect a frantic society."*
> —JEFF DAVIDSON

We dwell on earth at a time when more information becomes available in a day than we can ingest in the rest of the week or month, if not year, or decade! Although previous generations certainly had their hardships—no remote controls, no iPods, no drive-throughs, no EZ Pass, and, dare I say it? no Facebook—they were never confronted with the number of potential distractions that we face today. You may already know or sense that on many different levels.

Each Minute Is a Miracle

I name names in this book largely because I lack the imagination to disguise names and protect the innocent. Nearly thirty years ago, a spate of "one minute this" and "one minute that" books began appearing, the most popular being Blanchard and Johnson's *The One Minute Manager*. Self-starters know that only one minute's worth of downtime would be a godsend. O happy day! Building on the one-minute theme, this book offers sixty solid techniques (one for each minute in an hour) for becoming and remaining productive. The book is divided into six parts, with ten techniques in each part.

We start with the basics—adopting the right mindset. Change your underwear, change your current disposition. Adopt the right mindset, adopt more productive behaviors. These fundamentals, which have proven to be effective, build the foundation of easily initiated techniques, attitudes, and actions that help keep most work and life challenges under control. From there, you'll find a variety of techniques ranging from the profound (they seem profound to me) to the provocative. I think you'll be pleased to discover that *none* of the tips are of the "just do it" (ugh!) variety.

If one technique doesn't work, another one will. Unquestionably and necessarily, many of the tips offered are contradictory—for example, some advise tackling the tough issues first, while others advise tackling easy issues first. Such is human nature and the challenge of finding what helps to get you started. A strategy that proves effective may lose potency over time, and then it makes sense to try another approach. Does anything work forever? Okay, well, maybe ATMs do (but even they can run out of cash).

Depending on the task, your energy level, what you've previously employed, and a host of other factors too involved for me explore within the pages of this mercifully slim volume, sometimes one strategy will work *mahvelously* well for you, and sometimes just the opposite may prove more effective. The common denominator of all of the techniques, whether they conflict with an earlier one or are totally outlandish, semi-amusing, or utterly pedestrian, is that they will help you quickly break through logjams when it comes to starting on important tasks.

The great news is that self-starting is a habit that can be learned. Knowing that you want answers and results *now*, the techniques offered here are primarily on-the-spot strategies for getting into action. Used deftly and repeatedly, they can help you form new habits that will aid in keeping procrastination at bay. It takes insight and effort to change, but your odds of succeeding are excellent! Okay, they're a lot better than they were moments before you picked up *The 60 Second Self-Starter*. As you read these sixty tips, remember that I'm not writing to change the world; I'll tackle that in my next book. I'm writing to change you. This book will give you the impetus to get up and moving. Failing that, it will at least round out your collection of self-help books or make for great fireplace kindling on cold winter nights.

1 **Approach Your Task in a New Way** People are more likely to delay action when they perceive that something is difficult, unpleasant, or represents a tough choice. "Gosh, can't argue with you there, Jeff."

Much of what you may need to undertake to achieve a desired outcome may not please you while you're doing it. Jogging miles to reduce your waistline or saving more money and spending less will not necessarily make you feel better on any given day. One fine day, however, when your waistline is at the trim target you've chosen and you've become the svelte version of yourself, or your savings account has grown to a healthy balance, you begin to understand that less-than-pleasing means contributed to the highly pleasing outcome.

"We form habits and then our habits form us."
—RALPH WALDO EMERSON

One way to get started when you're stuck, particularly for work-related tasks, is to approach the issue from a different perspective. When Tom Wolfe, the novelist with those semi-dapper all-white wardrobes, was already past the deadline on an article for *Esquire* magazine, his editor gave him a wonderful suggestion. Wolfe was directed to write a letter to his editor, describing how he would approach the article and what he would put in it. So, he submitted a draft that started like a letter.

Sure enough, by eliminating the first paragraph or two and retaining the body of what Wolfe had written, the editor had the requisite material. Like Wolfe, you may not have trouble with a task, but simply with starting. By approaching your task in a different way, it may become a whole lot easier to handle. You will see clearly, now that the rain is gone.

Unblock Writer's Block

One of the tasks that makes many people's list of areas where they frequently procrastinate is writing, or more specifically, as in the case of Tom Wolfe, getting started on writing. Writer's block, a term that refers to little more than procrastination related to writing, hangs heavy over the head of many a would-be achiever. If writer's block is a problem for you, if you're having trouble getting through that project report or analysis the boss wanted on his desk last week, the following suggestions, which will be discussed throughout the book, will help you to get started:

Visualize yourself completing the last sentence. By visualizing the completion of your writing task, you can break out of the chains that hold you back and get started on the assignment. (See tip #6 on the power of visualization.)

Clear your workspace. Remove everything (see tip #14) except what's needed to write your document. People often have trouble writing because their office is a mess and not conducive to creativity. Recognize that during the time you're preparing a report or other assignment you need to tune out distractions. Working on a clear surface is an effective way to do this.

> *"Adversity has the effect of eliciting talents, which in prosperous circumstances would have lain dormant."*
> —HORACE

Outline your ideas. Producing a one-page outline, or writing as few as ten key words on a page, can guide you through the preparation and completion of an article. Devote a block of time to simply preparing report outlines or chronological sequences that can later serve as a useful tool when you're ready to write the full-blown document. (See tip #35 on novelist John Grisham's detailed outlines.)

Write for a few minutes. And watch what happens. Forget all the excuses. You don't really want to offer them, and who wants to hear them? Set an alarm for four minutes, sit down, and start writing. Often you'll find that you don't want to stop after a few minutes (see tip #40). Getting started is the key obstacle to writing productively.

Once you can master this "few-minute technique," you'll develop a habit that will blast the term "writer's block" out of your vocabulary. This technique is so effective that even if you can't complete the document at the initial sitting, you'll finish faster and more easily than you would have otherwise.

2 **Tackle Procrastination Head-On** Don't beat yourself up if you find yourself procrastinating a bit more these days. When faced with too many assignments or too many things to accomplish, procrastination is an all too common inclination for many people. Tasks that might normally seem mundane appear more difficult when there's too much on your plate.

By the way, there's too much on your plate.

Be honest with yourself and admit your procrastination. Say it in the mirror if that makes it more real for you! "Hello, my name is [state your name!], and I am a procrastinator." If you make excuses or rationalize why you're not getting started, you open up the door to even more delay. If you're honest with yourself and acknowledge when you are procrastinating, then you're closer to taking action. Even the teeniest action in pursuit of a long-term goal is far better than nothing.

When push comes to shove—and here comes a shove—sometimes your best approach to procrastination is to simply face it head-on by searching for what exactly is blocking you. What is the real reason you can't seem to get started? Many moons ago, in her book *Creative Procrastination: Organizing Your Own Life,* author Frieda Porat offered a host of reasons why individuals procrastinate:

- Fear of disapproval, failure, making mistakes, being wrong
- Sticking your neck out, being noticed, not being noticed
- Confronting the unknown, committing ourselves, exposing our inadequacies
- Taking on too difficult a task, getting into trouble, being less than perfect
- Being rejected, being on the wrong side, and getting criticized

Could it be that one or more of these issues ring true for you? If so, your quest is to find the root cause of that fear. Did something happen on an earlier project or on an earlier job, or even earlier in life, that is prohibiting you from getting back on the horse? Do you fear that you won't do a good enough job or that you'll fail if you try?

Keep in mind that if the task is vital, it's worth starting, even if you do fail. Allow yourself to have a less than gracious start. Proceed in the face of choppy progress. Expect nausea. Barf if you have to. The boat will still sail.

When facing a notable task, self-starters recognize that true and lasting accomplishments require high costs in terms of hours, energy, and commitment. (Hmmm . . . maybe procrastinating is not such a bad idea. . . .)

Give yourself periodic acknowledgment as you progress toward your final desired objective. Progress is not always even. Heck, is it ever even? Anticipate some level of breakdown and backsliding. Two steps forward and one step back is more often the rule than the exception.

Be gentle with yourself and cut yourself some slack, Jack. After all, if you made no attempt, your chance of succeeding would be zero, a perfect goose egg.

Perhaps you can't get started on something because you haven't identified some lingering issues that are impacting your feelings. Such issues might include:

- Having mixed feelings about the task
- Thinking a task is unnecessary or unworthy of you
- Resenting having to follow through on a promise because you weren't able to say "no" in the first place—"No, no, a thousand times, no!"

If you can identify some of the underlying reasons behind procrastination, you have a more decent chance of surmounting them than if you didn't articulate the issues to yourself. 'Fess up and win! When you can identify the root cause of your procrastination, ask yourself about the consequences of not getting started. If the consequences you will experience as a result of not initiating the task are minor, you probably will not get started. If you recognize that the consequences are significant, then get a move on!

Occasionally you procrastinate because the issue at hand *does not* need to be handled, and the consequences of not taking action are minimal. Hold on there, bro, I'm not introducing this observation as an easy way for you to rationalize delaying tasks and responsibilities.

I'm simply saying there are occasions when your hesitation is based upon sound reasoning, such as when the task you have been putting off:

1. Doesn't need to be done
2. Doesn't need to be done by you
3. Doesn't need to be done in this way
4. Doesn't need to be done now

It's worth making the determination.

3 **Redefine the Challenge** Have you ever seen Kenneth Branagh's movie *Henry V*? If not, get it on DVD! The enactment of a miraculous redirection in military history is worth it all. Greatly outnumbered by the French at the Battle of Agincourt, Henry offered a speech so stirring and inspiring that his troops fought with a vigor transcending that of which (notice my grammar) they previously seemed capable.

The king spoke of the glory of England and how history would look back on that day. By doing this, he reframed his troops' view of the forthcoming event as not merely a battle, with the odds stacked against them, but as one of the greatest encounters of history. Win or lose, his men would forever be remembered as the valiant soldiers that they were. And while that might not be true, he sure did get them fighting.

So, too, we hear of coaches who give halftime pep talks that turn their teams around and enable them to achieve victory. Or, at least we see this stuff in the movies.

Generally speaking, unpleasant tasks don't tend to get any more pleasant with the passage of time. Certain tasks that are delayed, such as cleaning out the stables, get *much* worse over time.

So, if you have to do something, you might as well take care of it now. There is often no advantage in putting off the task.

The problem most often arises when you perceive a task as difficult, inconvenient, or scary. This is when you are likely to shift into procrastination mode. If you reframe the task, however mundane it may seem, as something contributing to your long-term prosperity, growth, career advancement, or domestic tranquility, you'll be far more productive.

> *"What we love to do we find time to do."*
> —John Lancaster Spaulding (or Spalding, depending on your source!)

Ah, but you protest! "How can a mundane task be exalted?" Usually it's not the task itself that is vital but what the task represents, which could encompass:

- Keeping your word
- Displaying your professionalism
- Maintaining personal discipline
- Serving as a model for others
- Breaking past old barriers

Remember, even the smallest seeds can yield a bountiful harvest.

4 **Associate the Meaning with Something Larger** In the bestseller *All I Really Need to Know I Learned in Kindergarten*, author Robert Fulghum discusses a bricklayer who merrily goes about his business while other workers seem to be plodding. When this buoyant laborer is asked how he can be so cheerful toiling all day long in the hot sun, while his colleagues seem to be less than excited about their work, he says, "They are laying bricks; I am helping to build a cathedral to celebrate the glory of God!"

Who knows whether or not the story is true, or if the brick-layer was even sane. The point is that whenever you face a task you'd rather put off, find the greater meaning behind the task itself. Sure, some tasks you have been assigned may seem tedious and even uninspiring. Yet, your performance will surely affect your team, and what the team does will surely affect the division or department, which may affect the organization, which could conceivably affect society, ad infinitum.

On a piece of paper sketch out a simple diagram or flow chart of how your contribution impacts those around you, how their contribution impacts others, and so on. Keep that perspective in mind, and those mornings when you would rather not be at work will start to vanish.

In my own career I've written more than three dozen books, but you can bet the farm that on many mornings I didn't want to write a single word. I too suffer from bouts of procrastination. I confess! Fortunately, writing *this* book was so reinforcing that I had no mental roadblocks!

One way I've been able to blast through any potential road-blocks and be a self-starter is to contemplate how the comple-tion of a new chapter adds to my overall progress on the book. It means that I will be finished that much sooner. Yippee! More important, I will be honoring my obligation to the publisher with whom I have signed a contract. The publisher is waiting for my manuscript, so he or she can then assign the project to copyedi-tors, then production design staff, graphic artists, and so on.

The book needs to be published as scheduled, and everyone else in the book sales and distribution chain has to be able to go about their business (do their "thing") before the book can reach the hands, or screen, of lucky you. Ultimately, readers will benefit as a result of my valuable pearls of wisdom. None of this could happen if I sat at my office, in eloquent obscurity, drawing blanks about how to get started. When I relate the meaning of my work to the Poppa Bear–sized issues related to my progress, I have that much more impetus to begin.

Okay, enough about me. The types of tasks and projects that you handle in your career undoubtedly affect others. Come on, you know that they do. Identify those players and related issues, and you will have an easier time getting started, day after day, even when it would be oh-so-inviting to simply "put things off" for a while.

"Many are called, but few are chosen."
—MATTHEW 22:14

5 **Reflect on Past Achievements** Years ago when I moved to Chapel Hill, North Carolina, one of the first things I did was visit the Dean E. Smith Center. Named after the former Hall of Fame coach, it is where the University of North Carolina men's basketball team plays its home games.

Each of the 21,750 seats has an unobstructed view of the court. There are no posts, banners, or other visual impediments. The sound system is wonderful—no reverberation or static, simply the clear, crisp tones of the announcer. None of that muffled loudspeaker babble that you can never understand. The lighting is perfect, as is the scoreboard, the ventilation system, and virtually all other aspects of the facility.

Even more notable is what hangs from the rafters. No, not Duke players in effigy, although that may be worth exploring. I'm talking about the retired jerseys of former UNC basketball greats and the championship banners acknowledging successful seasons. You would think that having such banners installed would have been old hat to a coach like Dean Smith, who in his career accumulated 879 victories, second only to Bobby Knight's 902 victories.

Yet, whether it's an Atlantic Coast Conference regular season championship, tournament championship, NCAA tournament participation, second-round, sweet sixteen, elite eight, semi-finals, finals, or NCAA championship (which happened in 1957, 1982, 1993, and 2005), everything the UNC Tar Heels have accomplished hangs from the rafters for all to behold.

The coaches and athletics department at the University of North Carolina profoundly understand the importance of celebrating accomplishments both large and small. No team can be the NCAA champion or even the Atlantic Coast Conference champion all that often—annually there are many good teams vying for such honors. Whether he needed it or not, the banners reinforced Dean Smith's own victories, reminding him that doing well in his own conference, making the NCAA tournament, or proceeding far in it were all worthy of recognition.

> *"Everything in nature is a cause from which there flows some effect."*
> —BENEDICT SPINOZA

Those banners, hung neatly from the rafters, serve a continuing purpose to the present coach, team, and all associated with Carolina basketball. They tell new recruits, "We have a tradition here. We are winners, and we will win again." They remind current team members of the triumphs of recent years and help spur them on to earn yet another banner or two.

Okay, so how does this relate to you? If you have trouble getting started, dig up those letters of praise you received for previous projects or commendations you received for meritorious efforts. Think about the times you had trouble getting started in the past, what happened once you finally did get started, and how good you felt once you accomplished what you set out to accomplish.

When you can reread your kudos, or simply summon those same feelings of satisfaction, happiness, and accomplishment, you may well have the winning formula for getting started on a troublesome task. Did I tell you what a great reader you are?

6 **Visualize Yourself Succeeding with Ease** You hate public speaking and find yourself having to prepare for a banquet speech. Horrors. You continually put off working on your address because you've always been so nervous before a speech that you can't even wedge a morsel of dinner down your throat.

Visualization to the rescue! (And I don't mean visualizing the audience members in their underwear.) Undoubtedly you've read about Olympic athletes who have used visualization techniques to enhance their performance. Have you ever tapped into this powerful technique yourself? Using it, you can blast through your reticence to get started on your speech, or even combat long-term procrastination on lengthy projects.

Olympian Dwight Stones, a high jumper who represented the United States in the Olympics some thirty-five years ago, was one of the most avid and prominent users of visualization techniques in the sport. His method was so precise and so observable that he influenced the generation of high jumpers that followed him. You don't have to be an Olympic athlete in pursuit of a gold medal to engage in this process, but his experience in the Olympics is a good place to begin the discussion.

Before every jump, during practice or actual competition, Stones took his place a measured distance away from the high-jump bar and paused for several seconds. He then envisioned himself taking every step on the way toward his launch over the bar. During televised competitions, particularly the Olympics, you could see Stones moving his head up and down, seemingly counting the steps, as he visualized his approach and takeoff.

"Nothing is so fatiguing as the eternal hanging on of an uncompleted task."
—WILLIAM JAMES

When he "reached" the final step before the jump, you could see him contemplating the angle at which he approached the bar, where he'd plant his foot, how he'd use his arms and upper torso to create upward thrust. Sure it looked a little mystical, but the guy could jump! Stones's head movements told you in advance that he planned to clear the bar easily, land on his back in the proper position, and be pleased with his efforts.

Dwight Stones used such visualization techniques to help achieve record-setting performances. Certainly, he didn't clear the bar at every height every time. Many of his jumps were misses—he knocked over the bar and in some cases, failed to make the jump altogether. But, such misses and failed attempts are never the focus of visualization. Success is!

Likewise you can visualize succeeding at every step along the way to giving an effective speech, from writing it to arriving at the meeting site, approaching the lectern, not losing your lunch, speaking with eloquence, and receiving hearty applause. In this, and in virtually all professional as well as personal endeavors, employing visualization helps you to perform well and accelerate your progress. You accomplish your task in ways that non–self-starters, who don't use visualization, cannot appreciate. Too bad for them.

Be Like Mike

Here's a variation on visualization that may work for you: simple observation. During his heyday as a basketball player and ever since then, Michael Jordan has been paid a small fortune to endorse products. One of his earlier commercials offered the then-famous line, "Be like Mike." The advertising ploy was that if you bought and used this product, you could be like Mike, because he bought and used it too.

We certainly can't be like Mike was on the basketball court, but if we shine a little in the workplace like Mike, wouldn't that be a good thing?

When it comes to self-starting, is there a "Mike" in your office—not someone six feet, five inches, but someone widely regarded as having a take-charge attitude? This is the person who seemingly never procrastinates, at least not in a way that others can notice. This is somebody who "takes the bull by the horns" and dives headlong into complex tasks and demanding projects. You know, the exact opposite of the Cowardly Lion.

> *"We may affirm absolutely that nothing great in the world has been accomplished without passion."*
> —GEORG WILHELM FRIEDRICH HEGEL

Action-oriented role models are all around us; largely, they are the winners in life. We see them on television, in newspapers and magazines, even walking down the street. Although you previously may not have considered the value of studying the behaviors of action-takers and high achievers, now is the time, so get ready.

What can you learn by observing such role models in your office or anywhere else you find them? Discover how they launch into arduous tasks and blast through any feelings of procrastination. Summon up your courage and ask what makes them get started so quickly on challenging tasks. Glean from them any shreds of wisdom they will impart.

Hereafter, if you've been stalling on a project, consider one of the high achievers in your organization. How would the person act in the face of the task you're confronting? Sometimes simply envisioning this person and the kinds of action he or she would take is enough to get you started. *Be* like Mike, or Moby, or Mikhail, or Marianne, or anyone else whose action-oriented behavior is worth emulating.

7 **Experience the Fear and Proceed Anyway** Dr. Susan Jeffers, in her book *Feel the Fear and Do It Anyway,* discusses how tasks and activities outside of our comfort zones may cause us to feel uneasy. This discomfort is predictable—it is a typical human response to challenges that may seem a bit out of the ordinary.

Jeffers suggests that when you encounter a task that represents a hurdle or a roadblock, you need to let yourself feel all the emotions that arise. Are you uneasy? Quivering? Lightheaded? Is your stomach upset, are you trembling, or do you feel fearful?

When you're forthright with yourself about how you feel (namely, scared!), initiate your action anyway, Jeffers says. Often you're able to break through your fear and overcome the obstacle that loomed so large when you weren't being honest with yourself.

It is vital to recognize that fears about certain situations or tasks you face need not be debilitating. You don't have to hide underneath the covers when the big, bad deadline is out to get you. Indeed, if you allow yourself to feel the fear of whatever task you have been putting off, in whatever form the fear takes (facing penalties for missing a deadline, missing out on a one-time opportunity or investment, and so on), you actually position yourself to more easily begin the task at hand. So, get scared, and get started!

> *"Every day, in every way, I'm getting better and better."*
> —Émile Coué

Before a car's ignition will start, you need to turn the key, unless of course it's hot-wired. Before you blast through the procrastination, you feel the fear. When regarded as a routine, feeling the fear can become an important weapon in your arsenal. The next time you dread launching a new project, allow yourself to experience the full gamut of fear-related sensations. Feel the fear and start anyway.

If one of your underlying reasons for procrastination is the fear of success, then your immediate mission is to gain reliable knowledge of how this success would actually affect your career and life. You can talk to or read about others who have achieved similar success, or you can talk to associates and friends about the success. Or, simply sketch out on paper how you see the situation unfolding. Your guesstimates are as good as anyone's. In any case, get your thoughts down on paper; doing so helps deflate the fears and uncertainties.

Hereafter, rather than letting feelings of fear stop you, you may be pleasantly surprised to find how much easier it is to start. Indeed, you have passed the first step on your road to self-starting: you have felt the fear.

8 **Discard Limiting Language** Some words such as "must," "should," and "ought" seem a little less than positive. So do cuss words, but that's a different story.

If you were told by your parents, teachers, or coaches that you *should* do something, you *must* do something, or that you *ought* to do something, chances are that you regarded such exhortations as commands or burdens. As an adult, you unconsciously may still regard such terms with disdain, even when you use them in your own thinking!

I shall elaborate. If you think to yourself, "I must finish the ABC report by Thursday," you unconsciously may be regarding the completion of the ABC report as overly burdensome, sort of like making your bed or being nice to your sister.

Each time you think to yourself, "I should, I must, I ought to do something," the energy that you naturally have for such tasks is not nearly as high as it would be if you changed your internal language. Instead of thinking, "I must finish the ABC report by Thursday," replace that language with "I *choose* to finish the ABC report by Thursday," "I *want* to finish the ABC report by Thursday," or "I *will* finish the ABC report by Thursday." Instantly, your entire being realigns and re-energizes itself to aid you in your proactive choices.

Suppose you receive a call, and a customer or client requests a certain bit of information. Instead of saying, "I'll have to dig up that file for you," instead say, "I will be happy to locate that file for you." This conveys a more upbeat message to the caller. Even more important, it makes the task seem far less onerous for you.

Your use of language within the confines of your own thinking or conversation with others magically and rapidly transforms your ability to begin tasks of all sizes. Hereafter, if you find yourself reluctant to handle a task, employ language such as "I choose,"

"I want," "I will," and "I will be happy to," and notice the dramatic improvement in your energy and attitude!

"Okay Jeff, I will be happy to follow these suggestions."

"To know and not to do is not yet to know."
—ZEN PROVERB

9 **Engage in Creative Procrastination** Everyone procrastinates now and then, including the person in your seat at this moment, whether or not you care to admit it. It is part of the human condition. To make the best of a lingering case of procrastination, fill your time with efficient activity prior to getting started on the task you've been avoiding. Although you are not tackling the item that merits your current attention, you use this period of "creative procrastination" to take care of all those other things which you would eventually handle anyway.

Rather than simply frittering away the time when I procrastinate, I try to accomplish as many of the other small tasks as I can while putting off the big one that I know I need to be tackling. Too often, many people who procrastinate not only ignore the main task at hand but also fail to accomplish all the other little tasks that will eventually need attention. They dawdle. They surf. They hurl.

"Misspending one's time is a kind of self-homicide."
—GEORGE SAVILE

If you complete secondary tasks, eventually—when you're able to begin the major task and finish it—the major task *and* all the secondary tasks are done. Given that someone is not awaiting your completion of the major task, you're in the same place you'd be if the major task had been tackled first and the secondary ones last! So, just when you thought you were the master procrastinator, you were being productive after all! It's a form of time-shifting. The key is to continue to do things that are of some importance during your procrastination, rather than dilly-dallying.

Once you begin to tackle the larger project or assignment, you can approach it with the mindset that "I completed all of these other things and now the slate is clear to do a good job on this." Hereafter, if you simply can't get started on a project, undertake other secondary tasks that you'll need to do anyway. In that way, you're at least taking care of other useful business. Once you finally initiate and finish the big, important task you've been shirking, all of these smaller but necessary tasks will already have been done.

On occasion it is understandable and even desirable to do something else other than the task you had originally set out to accomplish, such as when short-term, high-priority tasks or opportunities arise. Don't beat yourself up over such incidences—they happen to everyone. When that "something else" is finished, you can return to the task at hand. It'll be waiting for you, 'cause it's not going anywhere by itself no matter how much you want it to.

10 **Watch What You Say to Yourself** In *What to Say When You Talk to Yourself,* author Shad Helmstetter says that 80 percent or more of your internal dialogue focuses on your shortcomings; that is, much of what people say to themselves is negative. That means that most of us, all day long, are internally saying things such as, "I didn't do that right," or, "My collar is off," "I should have never sent that e-mail," or, "I'm fat," or, "I didn't do this job well," or, "They're going to think I'm stupid." If anybody ever heard this stuff they'd think we had gone off the deep end.

What about giving yourself some positive messages? I mean, you can't possibly be *that* bad, can you?

These messages work particularly well when it comes to self-starting:

"I choose to easily complete this transaction."
"I choose to feel at ease in finishing this project."
"I choose to masterfully complete this task."
"I choose to be effective in all aspects of my job."

Suppose that you have to learn how to operate new equipment at work. It's taking you longer than you wanted or expected, and you're now totally stressed out. You'd rather put off the task than continue. You're probably giving yourself one of these messages internally:

"I can't stand this."
"I'd rather be anyplace else."
"I can't do this."
"Get me outta here."

You *could* be saying to yourself:

"I easily accept this challenge."
"I've mastered situations that were more difficult than this."
*"I am going to be more productive because I know how to use
     this to its best advantage."*
"By tomorrow this will be a piece of cake."

To make self-talk work for you, particularly for becoming a self-starter, be more conscious of what you say to yourself. If you have a hard time thinking of positive things to say to yourself, take time to generate a list of statements you can use, and either write them down or record them. Such a list will help you replace the negative statements that you more routinely offer yourself. By letting positive, self-boosting statements into your internal dialogue, you enhance the learning process, experience less stress, and feel far better about yourself.

> *"Be careful of what you say to yourself."*
> —SHAD HELMSTETTER

When in doubt about what type of positive self-talk to employ, self-starters think to themselves: "I choose to feel good about what I'm about to do" or "I choose to easily take appropriate action." The great news is that you only have to make these silent choices (people might stare if you say them aloud) when you're having trouble getting started and not taking action.

11 **Rethink Your Priorities and Supporting Goals** Priorities are the handful of things in your life or career that are important to you. Priorities are broad elements of life, and they often become misplaced somewhere within your daily high-wire, somersault-through-flaming-hoops balancing act. *In this society and in this era*, it is wise to have only a few priorities. If you have too many, you're not likely to respect each of them. At some point, too many priorities become paradoxical—only a few concerns *can be* of priority. Goals support priorities.

A single priority may have one or more goals associated with it. For example, if becoming supervisor is a priority in your life, you might set goals to get to work early, contribute as much as possible around the office, and speak to your superiors about any additional tasks that need to be done, and maybe compliment the right people here and there.

The choices confronting most individuals are often similar: career advancement versus a happy home life; income goals versus income needs; and social-, peer-, or employment-induced priorities versus individual wants or needs.

"If a man does not keep pace with his companions, perhaps it is because he hears a different drummer."
—HENRY DAVID THOREAU

A goal is a statement that is specific to what you intend to accomplish, and when. All the goal setting and attainment you ever fantasized or hoped for, however, won't be fulfilling if your goals don't support your carefully chosen priorities.

Your goals can change as old ones are accomplished and, of course, if some of your life priorities change. Here are some well-constructed goal statements:

"To work out for thirty-five minutes, three times a week, starting today."
Underlying priority: staying fit. And as a side note, notice I said *starting today,* instead of putting it off until tomorrow.

"To increase my annual income to $63,000 next year."
Underlying priority: attaining financial independence.

"To recruit four new qualified salespeople by the end of the next quarter."
Underlying priority: having the optimal size staff on board.

You can use the same procedure as you did for choosing priorities when choosing goals. The major difference is that each goal has to support a priority, and each priority is supported by at least one goal. Here are some poorly set goals. Tell me why (silently).

"To sell as much as I can in the next six months."
"To complete the study for my client."
"To be the best employee in the division."
"To be a more loyal Britney Spears fan."

Give up? They lack specifics and target dates. Imprecision in goal setting leads to missed goals. If you frequently find yourself procrastinating, often it's because your goals are not well defined. Study the most successful people in your industry or profession. You'll find that the majority are take-charge, confident, action-oriented individuals with clear priorities and supporting goals. In essence, they are self-starters. They know they can't remain productive if they are not making the effort to determine what represents their next best move. Hmmm, sounds a bit like chess . . .

12 **Stake Your Claim on a Task or Goal** There's a common misperception that a goal you undertake has to be your own, devised by you, set by you, and pursued by you. Oust that thought. Studies have shown that it's entirely possible for one person to set goals for another and to have the entire process work. In fact, this happens every darn day in sales organizations, where sales managers develop quotas for the sales staff, and it happens as often elsewhere.

The key element here is to have the person for whom the goal is set adopt the goals as his or her own. It's okay; it's not stealing. This is welcome news for parents, managers, or anyone else who has responsibility for the performance of others.

On a daily basis, when you claim ownership of the goal to complete a task or project, you organize yourself in ways that support that goal. When a goal is yours, you don't need as many external motivators, such as deadlines. Besides, for many of the long-term and continuing goals that you set for yourself, waiting until a minute before the deadline would be foolhardy. You can't accumulate vast sums of cash, lose huge amounts of weight, or finish writing all your reports at the last minute. (Well, not yet, at least . . .)

Stand Up to the Challenge

If it's easy for you to slough off the blame, disassociate yourself, and pretend you didn't have any input—all easily perfected skills—chances are you were never committed to a project in the first place. When you're willing to take responsibility for the outcome, whether good or bad, the project is yours. If others come along and ask who's responsible and you tell them that you are, then, for sure, the project is yours.

A wonderful gauge for determining whether or not you are steadfastly committed to your project is to think about a situation in which the goal is taken from you. Suppose you could no longer proceed down your chosen path. Suppose all activity in pursuit of a goal had to cease. Would you be outraged? Would you object? Would you fight for your right? Would you call in the SWAT team? If so, it's your goal.

> *"Those who make the worst use of their time are the first to complain of its brevity."*
> —JEAN DE LA BRUYÈRE

Alternatively, if you could take it or leave it, if you wouldn't be that upset, if it all would be forgotten by the next day, if it won't keep you awake at night, chances are it's not your goal. If you haven't claimed ownership, procrastination is predictable.

If a goal or a simple task or assignment was not originally your creation, perhaps you have some leeway in shaping it. There are plenty of things you can do to make the task more enjoyable and rewarding for you and ultimately make it your own goal. You may choose to begin with some easy entrance point (see tip #39). Perhaps you can tackle the job one section at a time (see tip #51). You might devise other methods for proceeding that enable you to retain some amount of control and sanity.

13 **Aspire to Be Organized** Do you think of becoming and staying organized as sheer and utter drudgery? If so, you're not alone! You don't see people shooting movies, writing Broadway plays, or producing hard rock albums on the topic (though I might be on to something here . . .). Yet it's an unheralded key to being productive. From pack rat to Jack Sprat to Jack Black, when you're in control of your surroundings, you have a better chance of staying focused, efficient, and effective.

"Don't let life discourage you; everyone who got where he is had to begin where he was."
—RICHARD L. EVANS

Everything you've ever filed presumably has future value, if only enabling you to cover your ample derrière. People often avoid filing because they don't see the connection between filing and its future impact on their careers and lives. Simply organizing materials, hard copy or on disk, putting them into smaller file folders, stapling them, or rearranging the order of things often represents a good, pre-emptive move in the battle against procrastination.

File, smile, and work in style. For each item that crosses your desk or hard drive, ask these fundamental questions:

- What's the issue behind the document?
- What does it represent?
- Why did I receive it? (This one is a biggie.)
- Why keep this? (Is it important? If it will be replaced soon, I don't need it.)
- Should I have received this?
- How else can this be handled?
- Can I delegate it? (See tip # 45)
- Can I file it under "Review in six months?"
- Can I shred it with glee?
- What will happen if I don't handle this?

Next, create a folder on your computer "desktop" and establish a physical drawer (make it a big drawer) where you can temporarily house what you want out of sight. Many people have inbox folders, which they label with months and weeks. It's a place to park things when you can't figure out what else to do with them.

You may ask, "Aren't I postponing my ability to deal with an overaccumulation of information? Aren't I throwing this in with the files I'm going to have to deal with in another three weeks?" No way, José, and here's why: When those three weeks roll around and you find the information you filed, the answer may take care of itself. You know it can be sent to the Recycle Bin or that it is more important than you first thought. Often, you get a definitive answer in a short period of time. You're not postponing dealing with the surplus—you're reviewing it at a better time. Out of sight, but not out of mind.

Eliminate clutter without a shudder. Then when you're in control of your information and files, you're able to retrieve items easily and use them, as opposed to having them buried and inaccessible for all eternity. In the meantime, you are not visually bogged down by such things, and you are also more prone to initiate action on the task at hand. Let's face it, we all know people with dozens—no, make that hundreds—of electronic file folders, housing thousands of e-mail messages. Likewise, we all know people with desks and file cabinets that are packed to the gills with over-stuffed file folders. Is this any way to manage your career? I think not!

One of the familiar laments among those who put off getting organized is, "I have never been good at organizing." All is forgiven. Start now, and you can do as good of a job as the next person. The only difference between people who are "good at organizing" and people who think they are "not good at organizing" is that people who are organized recognize that it takes some effort to maintain the organization. The people who are "not good at organizing" think they missed out at birth (or is that at conception?) on the "organizing gene."

Those who are "not good at organizing" further believe that somehow things mysteriously get out of order or become lost.

Many people even think that there are forces in the universe operating in opposition to them and conspiring to keep them disorganized. Get off it—you can maintain control of what crosses your desk and how it is handled. And I have news for you—your dog did not eat your homework, and that important document did not just sprout legs and walk away.

14 **Manage Your Desk for Performance** The quality and ambience of your work space is at its best when it demonstrates *the quality and ambience of your life,* or how you would like your life to be: rearrange your desk, change your life. Find your personal "zone." The zone is the place and space where you do your best work, where you are in the groove and where your work is exemplary. Procrastination has little chance here, even with you.

Joe Sugarman, in his book *Success Forces*, explains that by clearing your desk every evening, you automatically have to *choose* what to work on the next day. Though such reasoning is contrary to the advice of time management "experts," I wholeheartedly endorse it. It is a discipline that yields a marvelous ability to get started in the morning while others find themselves only slowly getting out of the gate.

To create my own "mini–desk workout," I keep some items on the far end of my desk so that I have to reach to use them. I fight procrastination, and I stretch my muscles!

What about inside your desk? Include frequently needed supplies, but remember: a desk is not a supply cabinet. Maintain a drawer of personal items—your desk is there to support you. Tissues or cough drops are okay. Sorry, your Game Boy is not. Include any needed forms or heavily used items, but leave a 20 percent vacancy. Constantly review what you're holding and decide to retain or toss it. Near, but not on your desk, go the familiar items such as pictures, plants, and motivators. Also, install any supporting accoutrements, from full-spectrum lighting to ocean wave music, if they support your productivity, efficiency, and creativity (and if your coworkers don't mind).

> *"Challenges are what make life interesting; overcoming them is what makes life meaningful."*
> —JOSHUA J. MARINE

To ensure that your desk and work environment support your productivity, *invest in yourself*. If you need them and can obtain approval from the powers that be, room dividers and sound barriers are available in a wide variety of shapes and sizes and can improve upon any existing sound barriers. The gentle, rhythmic "white noise" of a small fan's motor serves as a sound buffer to many of the sounds that may distract you.

Every evening after you've cleared your desk, congratulate yourself for what you accomplished that day. Don't do a number on yourself and beat yourself up for what you didn't do. Nothing would be accomplished, and you'd be in pain. It's likely that you're doing the best you can. If you can do better, you will—maybe not immediately, but soon enough, certainly by the next millennium.

So as previously recommended, do your filing and come up smiling. Use the end of the day, slow periods, or periods of low personal energy to revamp your files, keep your desk orderly, and better prepare yourself for high-octane output when you're ready to get started again.

After you've cleared your desk, apply the same principle to your computer's desktop, your inbox, the top of your file cabinet, closet shelves, and other areas of your life—your dining-room table, your car's glove compartment, the trunk of your car, and your health club locker (if not for better organization than at least for your personal hygiene). The fewer things you have in these places, the greater sense of control you have over your environment. Once these flat surfaces are under control, self-starters gain a heightened sense of control over their time.

15 **Set Up Your Desk for Decision** Given that you've gotten your desk under control, now go a step further. Set up your office to enable you to focus on the task at hand, and ignore other less important matters. This might involve neatly arranging papers, file folders, reports and other items, while working at a clear desk, with only the issue at hand in front of you.

Remember that simply having too much in your visual field can be an impediment to beginning a task.

"It is not necessary to change. Survival is not mandatory."
—W. EDWARDS DEMING

When you have only a single project or task at hand, your odds of maintaining clarity and focus increase dramatically. This is even truer if you're not in your own office or cubicle but at a conference table or at some other location at which you only have the project materials at hand.

Did you see the movie *Top Gun*, in which Tom Cruise plays a Navy fighter pilot? ("Your ego is writing checks that your body can't cash.") Among his many responsibilities in flying some of the nation's most expensive aircraft is landing those jets safely on aircraft carrier decks.

Months after seeing the movie, I read an article in *Smithsonian* magazine about how aircraft carrier decks are to be completely clean and clear before a plane lands. "All hands on deck" on an aircraft carrier means that everyone, even senior officers, needs to pick up a push broom and sweep the deck clear. The goal is to leave nothing on the surface of the deck, not even a paper clip, in order to ensure a successful landing. If there is debris on the deck as a plane approaches, or an earlier plane has not left the landing strip, the approaching plane is likely to crash.

Your desk is like the deck of an aircraft carrier. If you take the next pile of stuff you receive and park it in the corner of your desk with the notion that an organizing fairy will leave a nice, neat file under your pillow in the morning, good luck! Nobody's coming to help you manage your desk. Each new item you pile on will figuratively crash in the smoldering ruins of the accumulations in progress.

Get into the habit of managing your desktop as if it's important in enhancing your productivity—because it is. Don't let glut put you in a rut. Cut through the clutter like a hot knife through butter. If you only have whatever you're working on in front of you, and the rest of your desk is clear, you're bound to have more energy, focus, and direction. You're in a far better position to take action. The top executives of major corporations know this; that's why their desks remain clear and uncluttered.

16 **Get Your Ducks in a Row** It is reasonable to schedule time to take care of life's administrative tasks, such as handling correspondence, paying bills, straightening up, and keeping things in order. These activities can be as important as anything else in helping you attain your optimal performance level. They can prepare you to best tackle critical tasks and projects. Heck, the grounds crews take time to mow the grass and line the fields before every baseball game, so there has to be some sense in tidying up!

Some people find it advantageous to set aside a whole day solely for taking care of "administrivia." Thereafter, they have uninterrupted days of highly productive activity. For a specific task, when you know that there are going to be bottlenecks, you have a tendency not to get started. If you marshal your resources and take care of contingencies, you have a far greater chance of starting and staying with the project from the outset. Often it makes sense to handle minor tasks before tackling something larger.

If you know you're going to need support somewhere down the line, ensure at the outset that it will be forthcoming. This will help you get started on projects that you otherwise may find yourself lingering over.

You intend to come into the office Saturday (yeah, right!) to reorganize your now messy filing system. So, during the week, as you pass by retail stores, or the company supply closet, you accumulate file folders, hanging folders, identification tags, and a waste bin for documents you no longer need. This way, when Saturday arrives, you have no excuse!

"We first make our habits, and then our habits make us."
—JOHN DRYDEN

By assembling these items in advance—lining up your ducks—you all but ensure that you'll proceed at a productive pace on Saturday when you tackle the job you have been planning. If you buy too many garbage bags, bring too many folders, don't worry. You will use them eventually. Garbage happens. And you'll likely need even more in the near future. You are not likely to use all the glass cleaner either, but it will certainly come in handy for other windows at other times. As far as the bug spray, hopefully you *won't* need that again.

To not line up your ducks before starting a big project would ensure inefficiency, excessive downtime, and (need I say it?) further procrastination!

Lining up your ducks doesn't always equate to buying things. It may be as simple as assembling items that you already have at your disposal, such as that all-important duct tape. For work-related projects, lining up your ducks might entail identifying key resources in advance, such as phone numbers of contact people, URLs of vital Web sites, or a list of usernames and passwords.

Lining up your ducks complements plotting a course (see tip #35). Simply jotting down the items or resources that you might need in advance of tackling the project represents prudent time management, is comforting, and, in retrospect, almost always proves to be rewarding. Then, go have a life, at least for the rest of the day. It's rumored that time off can be quite enjoyable.

If you're in need of an effective scheduling system, these days there are software programs across the Web designed to help the organizationally challenged. The time management software for Windows, Achieve Planner, allows you to arrange tasks hierarchically and color-code your priorities. The distributors at *www .effexis.com/achieve/planner.htm* assert that this program will help increase your productivity. You can also identify others easily. The point is, find something that works for you and stick with it.

17 Live "in the Zone" Being "in the zone" is wonderful. You know about the zone—not the diet, but the place and space where you do your best work. Where you're in your groove. Where your work is exemplary. Where computer solitaire or FreeCell has little chance to derail you.

Regardless of what you call it, would it be useful for you to know how to get into the zone on a more consistent basis? You bet it would! Here's a simple exercise you can undertake to help create that environment in which you can work at your best.

Recall a time when you were highly productive:
- Where were you?
- What time of day was it?
- Was anyone else around?
- What was the temperature?
- What was the lighting?
- What resources were available?

Think about what you did at that time:
- What were you wearing?
- What did you consume the night before?
- How long did you sleep the night before?
- With whom did you sleep the night before?
- How did you feel?
- What was your level of fitness?
- What did you eat that morning?

Consider the time of day and week:
- What time of day was it?
- What day of the week was it?
- What had transpired earlier?
- What was forthcoming?

Think about the tools available:
- Were you using a computer or PDA?
- Were you using other equipment?
- Did you have a pen or pencil?
- Did you have a blank pad?

- Were you online?
- Were other resources available?
- Were periodicals, books, or directories present?

Assess other factors that were present:
- Did you have a view? (a room with a view!)
- Were you in a comfortable chair?
- Were you at a desk or at a table?
- Were you in a moving vehicle, such as a plane or a train?
- Was there quiet, or soothing, background noise?
- What were the colors of the walls surrounding you?
- Were you in a room with rugs?
- Could you hear others?
- Was water nearby?
- Were you near the bathrooms?
- Were you near the coffee machine?
- Was the coffee decent?

Circle each item in the previous list that was present or was a factor when you were in the zone. Undoubtedly, insights will emerge. Next, recall another similar experience and read through each of the questions once again. Which items have now been circled twice?

> *"Work joyfully and peacefully, knowing that right thoughts and right efforts inevitably bring about right results."*
> —JAMES ALLEN

If you can recall a third or fourth time in which you were highly productive, and run through the questions again, a strong pattern may emerge. You'll know which factors were present at those times you seemed to be highly productive. When they're stuck getting started on some task, self-starters emulate their zone scenarios to increase the probability of achieving great results.

18 **Decimate Distractions** Suppose you're working with your computer and the monitor starts fading. It flickers back on, then conks out for good. Bingo, your tension level rockets upward because this event is frustrating. You had a decent notion of what you wanted to finish that morning. Waiting around for your office's tech support staff wasn't included on your list. Office distractions and interruptions, in a word, suck.

> *"Half our life is spent trying to find something to do with the time we have rushed through life trying to save."*
> —WILL ROGERS

When you find yourself in an environment (or for that matter, a whole society) that subjects you to all manner of distractions and interruptions, even the smallest of tasks can loom larger. Sometimes the reason that you procrastinate on a project is that you anticipate interruption. To eliminate this possibility, eliminate distraction. It's like Terminix without the bugs.

To concentrate, you may have to escape from everyday events. For example, hold your calls, don't accept visitors, and forgo constantly checking e-mail. These distractions could be a reason for your procrastination, so eliminate them and give yourself some uninterrupted time. Yes, that means no Facebook or MySpace. If you're constantly tempted to surf the Web, check your e-mail, or play Spider Solitaire when you should be working, you might benefit from a program like Temptation Blocker, at *http://sourceforge .net/projects/temptblocker*, which enables you to "lock yourself out of specific applications" for the amount of time that you specify.

If you think the task will take an hour, make sure that you don't have distractions for at least ninety minutes. If you finish sometime between thirty and ninety minutes later, you can always re-enter "the world" as you choose. Occasionally, it makes sense to simply go to a private place, such as a soundproof room or bank vault, so that you can give your full attention to a particular task. (More on this in the next tip.)

Combating Distractions and Interruptions

Not surprisingly—to me, anyway—the single most challenging workplace stressor is interruption. From a list of more than fifteen stressors at work cited by managers, including work load, organizational politics, disciplining someone, dealing with upper management, balancing work and personal life, working within budgets, conducting performance reviews, and interruptions, you guessed it . . . interruptions was number one!

Years back, a study conducted by *Industrial Engineer* magazine found that the typical interruption sustained by managers lasted between six and nine minutes . . . bad but not crushing. Now hear this: The average time managers needed to "recover" from interruptions last an additional three to twenty-three minutes! Even if your math SATs weren't that great, you can quickly surmise that even a mere handful of distractions and interruptions per hour can flatten your productivity like a pancake. Is it any wonder that most career professionals consider interruptions to be the most stressful aspect of their jobs? Now throw 120 people into one large room separated by flimsy cubicles and I think you see where office productivity is headed.

Never mind the old adage, "It's so noisy, I can't hear myself think." Today, in some environments it's so noisy, you can't hear yourself speak!

I once consulted for a manager who supervised six employees. He sought to accomplish more on the job, but with each of his staffers coming to him with questions every couple of hours, he was at his wit's end. If each employee asked a question every two hours, in total the manager was asked an average of four questions each day, per person.

With six employees, that meant he fielded twenty-four questions a day, or 120 interruptions per week. This resulted in disruptions of the manager's work three times each hour in a forty-hour week! Now add in how long it took to "recover" from each interruption and, potentially, his whole day was consumed by distraction! Not fun.

I suggested a system to help him cope with the interruptions and to gain control of his time. I called it the J-4 System. (The "J" was for "Jeff." You can use your own initial.) I requested that the manager allocate the questions he received into four categories:

1. The answer to the first type of distraction, a J-1 type distraction, was already in print and did not need a personal reply from the supervisor (it was in the company policy manual or someplace similar). The manager could tell his staff people, "Please don't concern me with these kinds of distractions (J-1); go ahead and review materials you already have to find the answer."

2. A J-2 type distraction represented a question that a peer or bookkeeper could answer; the manager did not need to handle the question and could either quickly refer the employee to another person or ask that certain questions be taken directly to someone else.

3. J-3 type distractions required only a straightforward yes or no answer. These questions required interaction with the supervi-

sor, but not much—a quick phone call, buzz on the intercom, or beep on a pager.

4. Last came the J-4 type distraction. It represented a question that required the manager's input—one that he needed or wanted to, answer. "Yes, send it my way." "I'll handle it." "You bet I'm concerned."

In the course of a week, how many questions might be of the J-4 level of importance? Assume that each person asked two J-4 questions per day for a total of sixty interruptions each week. This cuts the number of interruptions in half! Actually, the manager achieved an even greater reduction because as time passed, his staff became more self-reliant and asked fewer question of all types, including J-4s. Equally important, he was able to better use his time.

If you'd like extra help minimizing distractions, you can download word-processing software that is distraction-free. Hog Bay software's WriteRoom for Mac OS and its Windows counterpart, Darkroom, hearken back to the old computer days, with black screens and green text. There are no fancy features to get in your way; "now it's just you and your text." As described at *www.hog baysoftware.com*, WriteRoom and Darkroom are "for people who enjoy the simplicity of a typewriter, but live in the digital world."

Once you have set upon a course of action, you tend to stay on that path. It is crucial that you devise some kind of strategy at the outset that will keep distractions at bay for the duration of the time you require. Too many people do a reasonably good job of eliminating distractions at the outset of a project. Thereafter, however, they let down their guard, then wonder why it's so difficult to achieve completion. Fortunately, you have the ability to move from constant distraction to focused action!

19 **Disconnect Yourself** Sometimes it makes sense to simply hole up somewhere so you can give your full attention to your task. When you have resolved that any disturbances in completing your task will not be tolerated, condition your environment for no distractions. Instead of going in to work, maybe you can work at home one day. You could barricade yourself in a room and post warning signs, take the far cubbyhole on the top floor, or find any remote location where you avoid distracting influences. Oh, wait, considering where you live, maybe you need to go to a hotel and book a room.

"I was taught very early that I would have to depend entirely upon myself; that my future lay in my own hands."
—DARIUS OGDEN MILLS

You want to move yourself totally away from others so that you have the opportunity to give your full attention to that which you want to accomplish. Often, you can accomplish in hours what otherwise might require a week because you're that good when you're not distracted!

Question: It sounds like a luxury to be able to allocate a block of time just like that. How many people can actually do this?

Answer: Nearly everyone has some discretion over how he or she will complete a task. If you have to leave your workplace for what you need to complete the job at hand, most bosses understand. After all, they're not paying you to procrastinate.

In advance, identify those places where you will be able to work steadily:

• A conference room
• A coworker's office

- A park bench
- The attic or basement
- A library
- A cabin at the lake
- The back porch
- A hotel room
- The car, while parked
- A picnic table
- An airport check-in line
- The children's tree house

You'll know when you've found the right spot. You'll feel good, productive, and unhurried.

Once you've found your location, you still may face the challenge of maintaining concentration. Someone once told me, "I'll get into a project, and I'll remember that I need to be doing something else." That's the procrastination phenomenon in full bloom: when you're tackling something that is difficult for you to tackle, undoubtedly you'll think of other things you have to do.

"Real glory springs from the silent conquest of ourselves."
—Joseph P. Thompson

Your task is to stay with what you chose to do at that time and let all the rest go. That almost sounds a little callous—to let all the rest go for the moment. Once you've gotten onto that big project that you've been putting off time after time—let's face it, you've let a lot of things go from time to time—you'll realize that being isolated helps!

Come on now, what better use of your time is there than to complete what it is you've chosen to complete?

20 **Begin Now, Which Is as Good a Time as Any** Many people believe that if they could only initiate tasks they've been delaying at the "right time," the tasks would be easier to begin and complete. For most tasks, there is no objective "perfect" time. I know of people who always wait until the top of the hour to start something, others who wait for a certain day of the week, and yet others who wait for a certain type of weather pattern! This is a self-deluding mind game. As much as you'd like to believe it does, the cycle of the moon does not determine when you should start your work. Give it up.

While there are work-related tasks for which starting at one time is preferred over starting at another, many of the tasks you face in the workplace could be tackled at this time or that with little repercussion. If you fill out your report log at 8:42 rather than 9 A.M. when it's not due until the afternoon, does it make any difference to anybody?

Do you believe that the IRS cares whether you initiated your taxes and ultimately filed them on February 27 at 10:36 in the morning or at 11:08? If you remove the clothes from the dryer before the news or after the news, are there any notable ramifications worth citing so long as no one is waiting for clean, dry underwear?

If you find yourself waiting for the perfect chance to begin a task, you're wasting precious time. You are a work in progress, and you can change. Let go of perfectionism. The project you've been delaying may not turn out perfectly. Follow through on your plan anyway.

For most of the tasks you face right now that you have delayed starting, the hard-core reality is that there is no perfect time to begin. In many cases, the "perfect" start time is simply another in a long line of tricks that your mind plays to make it seem as if there are legitimate reasons for not getting started.

Once you acknowledge that most tasks have no perfect start time, you may recognize that the best time to begin could well be right now! If you find yourself caught in the bind of waiting for a perfect time, such as when the weather changes or when you feel more like doing it, consider that for virtually all indoor tasks, the weather is arbitrary. As for waiting for when you feel like it—"feeling like it" is a state of mind that is under more of your control than you might suppose. When will you ever actually feel like cleaning out the hamster cage? The longer you wait, the dirtier it gets, whether you feel like it or not.

When people receive a check or a complimentary letter in the mail, they often regard that as a good day. Suppose the check or the letter came the day before or doesn't come until the next day? Determining that one day is better than another because of some external event is part of human nature. Yet, whatever you did to earn the sum or merit the letter was put in motion before the day you received it.

So too, it is erroneous to believe that there is a perfect time to start on tasks. The mental energy you need to put toward a task may already be working for you, long before the time you think is perfect for beginning. Often, the first moment you can start a task is as good a time as any.

When you talk to people who finally finish a project that they have been putting off, all the mental claptrap about the "perfect time" to start falls away. The act of getting started often makes that moment the perfect time. So, like a "good day," the concept of a "perfect time" is illusory. When you are able to engender positive feelings—when you get that warm tingling feeling all over—it is a good day. When you are able to begin an important task you have been putting off, it is a perfect time.

21 **Explore the Power of Scents** To begin Part 3, I will boldly go where no procrastination book author has gone before and introduce an age-old way for enhancing performance and productivity that will seem too "far out" to some readers and/or too leading-edge to others. Tip #6 discussed visualizing your way to success; here, you *smell* your way. Think about the last time you were in close proximity to the fragrance of your significant other. How did you feel when you experienced that scent? Scents are powerful and often more action-inducing than you might realize.

The mere scent of an orange peel, for example, may help you reduce mood swings and feel better about your day. Dentists have found that when they scent their offices, patient resistance and fear seem to diminish, right up until they hear the sound of the dentist's drill. Even patients having root canals, when immersed in a room primed with relaxing scents, exhibited less anxiety and higher levels of relaxation than those in unscented rooms (could you drill a little deeper, doc?) They even reported pain sensations less frequently. Toucan Sam has the right idea: "Follow your nose!"

If root-canal patients can experience these benefits, you can certainly smell your way to higher productivity. As our lifestyles adapt to a more fast-paced and technological age, we have to find a way to stay happy and balanced, yet competitive and productive. We have to stop seething and begin breathing. With more people spending long hours working at computers, we have encountered problems including eyestrain, heart disease, depression, lower back pain, and sore rumps.

Smell, more than any other sense, is the quickest way to change a mood. Studies have shown that specific scents can alter moods and behaviors. The evidence is found in measurable indicators of mood and emotion, such as blood pressure, heart rate, and body temperature.

Aromatherapy works by affecting the neurological functioning of the human body. Bath and body stores have made a killing exploiting this phenomenon. The limbic system in the brain is involved with the sense of smell and works closely with the nervous, respiratory, circulatory, and immune systems. The limbic system deals with memory, learning, and emotion. Relax, you don't have to remember any of that, only this: some scents can put you in high gear!

"He who loves the world as his body may be entrusted with the empire."
—Lao Tzu

Inhaling aromas stimulates the neurons of the brain. Upon entering the nasal passage, the essential-oil molecules stimulate the olfactory nerve, and messages are sent to the limbic area of the brain. This triggers physiological changes through the nervous, endocrine, and immune systems, and also in your lungs. Then the essential-oil molecules are carried to every cell in your body via your bloodstream. And if you're not up on your science, after different essential oils enter your body, they can affect you in different ways.

More than 300 essential oils exist, and it would take an entire book to describe what each one does. The following list is not complete by any means, but it can help you get started. As you can see, many of the essential oils and herbs fall into more than one category because they have more than one use. You have to find what works for you. If you try an essential oil that is supposed to have a specific effect, and you do not like the smell of it, don't use it any more. If you hate coffee, you don't have to wake up and smell it.

Effect	Essential Oil
Antidepressants	Bergamot, geranium, lavender, patchouli, rosebuds, rosemary, sandalwood, St. John's wort, ylang-ylang
Courage	Cedar, musk, rose, geranium
Harmony	Basil, gardenia, lilac, narcissus
Insomnia	Lavender, narcissus
Peace	Benzoin, cumin, gardenia, hyacinth, magnolia, rose, tuberose
Relaxation	Catnip, chamomile, frankincense, hops, lavender, rosebuds
Stimulants	Lavender, lemon, verbena, patchouli, peppermint, rosemary

And now, for the opposing viewpoint: Some skeptics question the validity of aromatherapy and contend that the effects are psychological. In other words, they claim that people feel better simply because they believe that the essential oils have therapeutic effects. Others point out that it doesn't matter why aromatherapy makes people feel better—it only matters that it does. So if you find an oil that uplifts you, stay with it!

If trekking to health-food stores for a few scents is not your cup of tea, at least recognize the importance of having your work environment support you. Surround yourself with plants, which convert nitrogen to oxygen, ensure that the ventilation is more than adequate, and have plenty of water nearby. I keep a water glass close at hand. For me, dehydration, more than anything else, is the key factor for low productivity. In half of the cases when you think you're too tired to get started on something, you're actually only thirsty.

22 **Tune In to Motivating Music and Messages** You can visualize yourself succeeding, smell your way to success, *or* listen your way to accomplishment. Whatever procrastination hurdle you face, you have a vast array of options for listening your way through it. If you have a CD and/or tape player in your car, or commute carrying an MP3 player, you can achieve some measure of control over your environment to and from work. Interested so far?

"The longest drought will end in rain."
—Robert Frost

Why not take supreme advantage of this time by listening to messages that will prompt and inspire you to take action?

You can listen to Books on CD® (*www.booksontape.com*) and similar services via subscription or by visiting your local library, which may also offer lectures, motivational programs, and books on CD and cassette. Apple's iTunes also offers many books in digital format. SkillPath, Nightingale-Conant, and Dartnell are the leading producers of programs on topics such as self-improvement, leadership, sales, and career advancement. (Hey, maybe someday you can listen to this book on CD!)

If your one-way commute is only twenty-five minutes, in eleven weeks, believe it or not, you could listen to the equivalent of a college-length course. In a little more than a year, you could achieve the equivalent of having audited five college courses—an entire semester. In time, you could be up there with the Ph.D.s. And all you wanted to do was get out of the rut you've been stuck in!

The beauty of such listening experiences is that you get to pick what you want to hear, you make an otherwise meaningless commute meaningful, and there are no quizzes, term papers, or final exams!

When faced with a task I've been putting off, I've found some recorded programs to be so stimulating that not only do I blast through the current bout of procrastination, but I sometimes end up setting even higher-level goals and stretching for even greater challenges. (Note: For a variation on using recordings, see tip #43.)

23 **Unshackle Yourself from Too Much Information** I frequently get phone calls after hours, usually around dinnertime, from nice people who start their canned pitch by saying, "Hello, Mr. Davidson. How are you this evening?" What does Jerry Seinfeld say when he gets a phone call at night, after hours? Mr. Seinfeld says, "Hey, why don't you give me your phone number, and I'll give you a call tomorrow when you are having dinner."

One night I got this call from a fellow, and just to be charitable, I decided to listen for a few minutes. He was from a brokerage house and had all these investment plans he wanted me to consider. Finally I blurted out, "Wait a second. Please don't tell me about your thirty-five investment plans. Boil it down for me. I never volunteer to be slimed" (to use the *Ghostbusters* term). "Tell me about the three investment plans that you think might be right for me."

After some hemming and hawing he finally agreed that he'd send me information on the three, not on the thirty-five he had planned to send. He then went on to tell me about the annual report his company just came out with, as well as the quarterly reports, which he could send along.

I told him, "No, no please. I don't need to read those reports. If I want them I can always call you back, I can look on the Internet, I can write to your company, or I can use the reader services features of *Forbes* or *Fortune*. There are many, many ways that I can get ahold of your annual report if I want to. Please, don't send your annual report or your quarterly report." And after a while he finally relented and agreed not to send his annual report or his quarterly report.

Then he went on, and I'm not kidding here, to mention his 10K—you know, the comprehensive report that public companies have to file with the SEC—and we went through the same routine. And then, *incredibly*, he talked about other lavish pieces of literature, all of which I didn't need. Was I talking to a wall here?

I spent eight minutes on this phone call simply convincing him that if he wanted to do business with me, the best way to reach me was to give me a slim little packet of maybe the three things that might work based on what he knew about my situation. He agreed, and I wondered what he might actually recommend.

I put down the phone and went about my business, and I totally forgot about it. After about four days passed, I got a package in the mail from his brokerage house. It was thick. No, that's not accurate; it was very thick—more than three-quarters of an inch. What was in the package?

I have no idea. Recognizing the name of his brokerage house, I knew that the package was way too large based on our discussion. I took that package, and with my powerful wrists, I tried to tear it in half with one mighty rip, but it was a Tyvek envelope— you know, the kind you can't tear—so I tossed the whole thing into the circular file. I won't deal with that broker, and probably not that brokerage house either. They overwhelmed me, and I specifically asked them not to. I never responded, never spoke to the guy, never had further contact. But you know what? If he had sent me that thin package, I might have made his day. And who knows? He might have made me rich.

Every other time, when I receive a large packet of information, I quickly break it down to the few pages that I might need. I use the edge of a ruler to quickly but neatly tear out only the bits of information that I want from each page. Then I quickly assemble such tidbits on the copier and create a one- or two-page composite of what might have been many, many more pages. It's my own form of "cut and paste." This affords a quicker review in the future, keeps my files leaner and more targeted, and is anxiety-reducing.

What about the case in which too much data related to a key decision is holding you up? Many people believe they need reams of data before making a go-ahead decision, and so they procrastinate. In an overly informed society, regardless of whether you're making a purchase, hiring someone, or opening a drive-through restaurant, you'll find enough information to persuade you to go both left and right. Often, you'll find so much information that a clear-cut decision is nearly impossible. Yet, more data does not necessarily produce the best answer, so don't let data overload contribute to procrastination.

A study was completed on the use of information in making decisions. Two groups of individuals had to make purchase decisions. One group's members were given data, analysis, and articles—everything they thought they needed. The other group made the decision based on instinct. After a few weeks, the two groups were able to see the results: The group that felt better about its decision had chosen on instinct!

"The art of being wise is the art of knowing what to overlook."
—WILLIAM JAMES

If you are forty years old, forty years of data is brought to bear when you make a decision. Instinct, then, is not based on a moment's whim—it's everything you've ever learned during your existence. Each of us has the ability to make intuitive choices, but for many, the words "intuition" and "instinct" are taboo. Yet the top CEOs of large companies often make decisions based on what feels right. Even Bill Gates goes with his gut feeling sometimes—and look at where it got him!

In a *Time* magazine article following the Persian Gulf War, Colin Powell said that one of the reasons he was able to make effective decisions in his military career was that he would wait until he had about 60 percent of the data that he could amass for a decision and then make his choice based on the data, his experience, and his instinct, rather than wait for all the "hard" information. Change your relationship to information. More data is not always the answer, especially in a society that deluges us with data. Enough data exists to lead to all possible answers, which clearly gets in the way of choosing.

Hereafter, give yourself the opportunity to get started on projects more quickly by relying more heavily on your internal decision-making apparatus! You have one, I promise.

24 **Ask Yourself, "Will This Ever Ease Up?"** I've long employed a question that has helped me tackle a vast array of tasks and projects that I would have rather put off. The question is, "Will it be any easier later?" The frequent answer, as *Top Gun* fans will attest, is, "That's a negative, ghost rider, the pattern is full. . . . "

For example, suppose I receive mail from a professional group to which I belong. The group is asking me to participate in a brief survey. My inclination may be to chuck the request because I'm busy. Heck, who isn't? Maybe I'll park it someplace and return to it later when I "have more time" or am in a better frame of mind to handle the task. When there's a mountain of unanswered mail in your path, your natural reaction might be to run in the opposite direction. These types of minor tasks mount up. Each one then perceptibly becomes an even larger burden than if you simply handled each as it arrived.

> *"The doors we open and close each day decide the lives we live."*
> —FLORA WHITTEMORE

In the case of a professional survey that I've been asked to complete, I ask myself the key question, "Will it be any easier later to complete this survey?" Often the answer is, "No." So, there and then, I read through the page or two, check the appropriate boxes, fold up the page, put it in the reply envelope, and immediately send it back. By doing this, I have experienced several small benefits:

- I have no mental "clatter" about the task.
- I did not park the survey someplace where I would have to retrieve it later.
- It did not contribute to a pile of other uncompleted minor tasks.
- The task never made my "to-do list," hence saving time.
- Achieving a quick completion on the spot helps me feel productive.
- The ability to quickly respond to minor requests has helped me to develop a reputation as someone who is a master of completions. People phone or write me expressing thanks for handling their requests so quickly.
- I can give myself a smiley-face sticker. . . .

These benefits spring from the simple acknowledgment that if it will not be any easier to handle a task later, the easiest time to handle it may well be now. In this case, "a stitch in time saves ninety-nine." "Later" requires that you reacquaint yourself with the task, which in itself requires mental energy. And who has any of that to spare?

Is there a letter or e-mail that you need to respond to? Will it be any easier or ultimately more beneficial to handle it later? If so, put it off until later. If not, handle it now. Especially in the case of e-mail, when simply hitting the reply button transmits your answer, it can be to your benefit to deal with the task now rather than later. If you need to make a phone call, will it be any easier to make it later? If so, feel free to put it off, but if it won't be any easier to make it later, then do yourself a huge favor and make the call now. You don't have to be wearing Nike to "just do it."

25 Recognize That Wanting Is Different from Deciding

Suppose a particular project is staring you in the face and you know there is no way you want to start it, now or ever! Because of whatever circumstances, the project is something that you have been assigned or otherwise have to accomplish.

Here is welcome news: *Deciding* or *choosing* to start on a project is quite a different state of affairs than *wanting* to start on a project. Like the professional who doesn't need to wait until he or she is in the mood to do a job (see tip #27), so too, you may not prefer to start on a project, but that has nothing to do with your decision to get started.

> "Opportunity may knock only once, but temptation leans on the doorbell."
> —ANONYMOUS

As you learned earlier, a change in language (see tip #8) can make all the difference in how you approach a particular project.

What you "should" do is not nearly as invigorating as something you will "be happy" to do. Likewise, choosing to or deciding to start on a project liberates you when you don't necessarily "fancy" starting a project.

"Ah, but this is merely semantics," you say. "You are playing with words. Can that help me blast through procrastination?" Quite a bit. Researchers have found that we actually think in language. That is why people who exclusively speak Bulgarian or Farsi or English or Gibberish think differently from one another. So too, subtle variations in the words we choose result in differences in our ability to translate thought into action.

The bottom line: If you have an important project due, forget about whether or not you want to start on the project, and simply decide to.

26 **Find a Buddy** Some tasks are simply too challenging—you can't face them alone. Two, four, six, eight, you need to affiliate! Seek to work with people who are facing a similar challenge. Is there somebody trying to accomplish the same task? If so, you have the perfect person with whom to join forces. Being a self-starter doesn't have to mean working alone; finding someone who has the same goals as you and is experiencing similar roadblocks can be a great advantage. Having a short-term partner, or at least someone with whom you can commiserate, yields significant benefits (see tip #44 for long-term partnerships).

Many people find that working alone is more difficult than working with others. If you see accomplishing a task as a lonely process, especially for those tasks with highly unpredictable results, you're more likely to procrastinate. Having a partner could be an antidote. There's safety in numbers!

When the blind leadeth the blind, get out of the way! The scenario of two partners in a similar struggle, however, is more than simply a case of the blind leading the blind. You can serve as sounding boards for each other, as in this case you are each more empathetic than anyone else around. The benefits of sharing a difficult ordeal with others are well established. People meet in groups such as Alcoholics Anonymous, Parents Without Partners, and Mothers Against Drunk Driving for support, insight, and commiseration.

For professional or personal tasks, your challenge becomes one of finding the right partner at the right time. Partners come in many varieties and under many different labels. Anyone described in this pantry of terms may prove to be a resource for you:

- Affiliates
- Friends
- Partners
- Comrades
- Team members
- Colleagues
- Principals
- Co-venturers
- Joint venturers
- Cohorts
- Collaborators
- Classmates
- Helpmates
- Compadres
- Mates
- Prison mates
- Crew members
- Staff members
- Founders
- Cronies
- Contributors
- Associates
- Helpers
- Accomplices
- Conspirators
- Group members

If you happen to attend a conference or convention populated with others in your industry, seek out those with whom you can network. Collect the business cards and e-mail addresses of people in other divisions of your own organization, or in entirely different organizations, who have responsibilities and challenges similar to your own. Whatever type of industry or group you belong to, you may find it to be a source of valuable allies in helping you succeed. Such groups include:

• Band	• Commission
• Team	• Ruling council
• Crew	• Board
• Union	• Advisory board
• Unit	• Committee
• Assembly	• Tribe
• Conglomerate	• Parliament
• Party	• Cabinet
• Council	• Congress
• Task force	• Clique

When you have at least one good affiliate with whom you can share insights and ruminate on the state of the universe and to whom you can pose questions, you are less likely to find yourself stuck in ruts. Quicksand can't stop you when there are inspired muses all around you. Whenever you can find someone who's up against the same challenges you are, you have the potential to increase your probability of achieving your goal.

If you can't find an affiliate, there may be someone at your workplace or within the organization who can simply talk to you for five or ten minutes to get you started. There has to be someone who likes you. If your ignorance on a subject is holding you back from starting or completing a task, find someone knowledgeable, and ask him or her for help. If the Beatles could ask for a little help from their friends, so can you.

Particularly for tasks that seem overwhelming, finding some-one who is knowledgeable about the situation and can give you a running start can be as good of an incentive as anything. Okay, anything within reason. When your questions are answered and you feel more confident about the task, you reduce the likelihood of procrastinating. Once that guide person leaves, keep on track with that task!

27 **Don't Dally Because You Aren't "In the Mood"** "In the Mood," written and conducted by Glenn Miller, was a popular song in 1940—just a little before your time. In affairs of the heart, being in the mood can make all the difference. Waiting until you are in the mood for work, however, can be a waste of time and a poor excuse for not getting started on the task at hand.

A generation ago, film stars who "weren't in the mood" were given substantial leeway as they stormed off the set (think Marilyn Monroe). Today, you rarely hear about such instances. The film industry is highly competitive, budgets are tight, shooting sched-ules are meticulously planned well in advance, and investors expect compensatory returns for their risk. Actors today are expected to perform on cue. And there is no room for drama queens. The notion of waiting until you are in the mood is antiquated.

> *"We are what we repeatedly do. Excellence, then, is not an act, but a habit."*
> —ARISTOTLE

For professionals, the reality of today's world is that waiting until one is "in the mood" is a luxury that most people cannot afford. Service professionals normally can't afford to wait until they are in the mood to dispense their services. Suppose you're a psychologist, with a full slate of clients booked for the day. How would they respond if you said to each one, "I can't go ahead with our appointment right now; I'm not in the mood." If you are a professional boxer, do you have the option of waiting until you are "in the mood" on the night of the big bout? No, because you'll get knocked out or lose an ear, depending on whom you're fighting.

Do you know the difference between a professional writer and an amateur? The professional writes on schedule whether or not he or she is in the mood. The amateur waits until he or she is in the mood, and predictably writes precious little (and mostly little that is worth reading). Across the broad spectrum of society, from presidents of countries to clerical workers, true professionals proceed onward independent of their emotions and feelings.

Now, about you. Undoubtedly you have to perform, often on cue, regardless of your mood at the particular moment. On deadline at the office, if you're not in the mood to handle XYZ, so what? Do you not accomplish great things all the time when at the outset you weren't in the mood? Of course you do. It is no different for tackling virtually any task you have been putting off at work.

Muster the impetus to start, and you'll probably do fine. Whether or not you are in the mood will soon become irrelevant. Taking action usually proves to be invigorating, so your mood will positively change anyway. Hereafter, don't let the "mood" issue arise at all when it comes to getting started on projects. It is a dead issue; give it a decent burial. May it rest in peace.

28 **Take a Flying Leap** Suppose your car breaks down on the side of the road, and you jump-start the battery. All of a sudden, the engine is revving. This is certainly not a time to turn the car off—you want to keep it on for a good twenty minutes.

Like a car on the side of the road, often all you need is a jump-start so that you can stop procrastinating and start moving again. This method of self-starting is much easier than tackling some difficult portion of your task first. The mere gesture of turning on your PC, popping a disk into the CD player, or flipping on your pocket recorder may be enough to get you started on a task that you have been putting off.

"Let him who would enjoy a good future waste none of his present."
—ROGER BABSON

The sound of your PC booting up may give you encouragement. Or it may be nearly inaudible in that noisy office of yours. Whatever task you're trying to tackle, find some element of it that you can complete quickly and easily. And it doesn't get much easier than pushing the power button.

In essence, flipping the "on" switch of your PC, having it boot up, and perhaps opening the appropriate folder and file, is analogous to jump-starting your car.

Likewise, once your PC boots up and your hard drive is humming, you may experience a jump-start in your ability to delve into the project. As a bonus, jump-starting often enables you to capture your first, and sometimes best, thoughts.

Just for you, here's a second form of jump-starting. When a new software program is introduced in your office, do you immediately jump into the fray, exploring its attributes—like a dweeby, *Star Wars*–obsessed techno-geek might do? Most people are not so inclined. Keeping in mind the value of getting help (tip #26) and in getting a jump-start, look to the "techies" among us who have an advantage in this department. You can draw upon their expertise and inclinations to help you blast through procrastination, particularly when it involves tasks related to technology.

Suppose you have to learn some new software or master some new piece of equipment. You dread doing it. Your inclination is to delay. Don't do as I used to do: spend endless hours in front of a PC, with the software instruction manual in hand, starting and stopping, presuming that I could suddenly become adept at skills for which I have never shown any significant potential.

If you can find someone who is good at this kind of stuff and can help you iron out the rough spots, then what might have been a personal ordeal may suddenly seem much more palatable. In my own career, I now steadfastly refuse to open software instruction manuals. I have college students as helpers. Some of them major in "computer science," or whatever they call it. They help me navigate through the maze of new software. We establish sequences and routines that I can follow. We type those "instructions" onto my hard drive and save them in a file I can easily access.

Rather than becoming enmeshed in all the features of a new software program, I instead focus on mastering the handful of capabilities that I want to use. As I become more familiar with the software, I ask my college helpers "what if" questions. What if I wanted to do this, what if I wanted to combine that, what if I wanted to eliminate this? What if I want to massacre my PC with a sledgehammer—what would it cost to repair? Then we discuss the options—with software there is always more than one way to proceed—and we find the path that best suits me, and bingo, I'm in action.

We then write and save the instructions in a master file of all the other instructions that I have saved. I have honed and refined this process and now am hardly ever at a loss as to how to proceed. No meandering, no procrastination, no having to deal with "geek speak." I now have regularly scheduled guides assist me with the various cumbersome, tedious, and frustrating tasks I encounter in work and in life.

Likewise, if you find yourself procrastinating when it comes to getting started on a project related to software, technology, or anything else in the office, find that knowledgeable, trusted trail guide who can give your motivation and your project a jump-start.

29 **Preview Your Taste** As a variation on jump-starting, give yourself a preview. Suppose you know you have to tackle a project on Monday, and you're dreading it. How can you make the project more palatable days beforehand? An effective maneuver is to review the project contents before the weekend. You might look over any supporting items, jot down some notes, begin a rough outline, or undertake other supporting activities now, while it "doesn't count."

The Friday afternoon before the project starts, your ideas and thoughts can flow freely. This ten-minute period can be valuable in facilitating your progress Monday, when it does count. Over the weekend, you don't have to do anything. You are allowed to be an absolute waste of space, the ultimate couch potato. Regardless, your subconscious starts working on the project. Knowingly or unknowingly, you're already going into the germination state, sprouting new ideas or letting a plan take root, and all from the comfort of your recliner.

When it's time to start the project on Monday, you'll find that you can actually get started with greater ease than you anticipated. The early preview is the key. Hereafter, if you have to tackle something on Monday that you've been putting off, briefly view the project on Friday so that when you return to it you have some semblance of familiarity with the particulars. This can also work during the middle of the week, before you leave for vacation, or sometimes even before lunch—certainly anytime when there will be a few days or hours between when you preview the item and actually work on it.

> *"I owe all my success in life to having always been a quarter of an hour beforehand."*
> —HORATIO NELSON

I've always relied on the kindness of my audiences. A fellow speaker who had heard me lecture on this topic sent me an e-mail of praise following her jump-starting success story. It seems she awoke in the middle of the night and couldn't get back to sleep. Recalling what she had heard at my presentation, she grabbed the folder of some project she would be working on later that morning and reviewed it while awake in bed.

After a while, she drifted back to sleep. In the morning, she reports, when she reopened the project folder, she was pleasantly surprised at the ease with which she began working. Her late-night preview served as an effective jump-start for her progress in the morning! What a deal.

30 **Take On the Hard Stuff First** Here's a short tip to close this section, and you look as if you could use a short tip. Sometimes a technique that works for you goes flat. In that case, it makes sense to try something else, perhaps even the opposite of what you've done previously (and the opposite of several of the tips already offered). I know it sounds like heresy, but battling the wily coyote named procrastination sometimes calls for some crafty moves. It's a dog-eat-dog world out there. Don't get caught wearing Milk-Bone underwear.

If you have control over the order in which to tackle steps, handling the seemingly unpleasant elements *first* may prove to be a workable strategy for you. If you do what you like first and save the unpleasant things for last, the probability of procrastinating increases. You don't want to let procrastination prevent you from your successful conclusion. When you handle the unpleasant tasks first, you diminish the possibility of procrastination becoming an issue.

> *"Hard work is often the easy work you did not do at the proper time."*
> —BERNARD MELTZER

Hereafter, anytime you have control over the order in which you tackle steps on the way to achieving a task, attempt to handle the seemingly unpleasant elements first. If you don't, and if you practice the converse—doing what you like to do first, and saving the unpleasant things for last—the probability of procrastinating increases and your chance of succeeding is about the same as the Cubs winning a World Series in this century. Sorry, Chicago fans.

Come Out Charging

31 **Make a Choice** Here's the "how" about living for now. Robert Fritz, founder of Technologies for Creating, teaches that by making choices and positive affirmations regarding what you want, you move closer each day to realizing what you want to accomplish. Making deeply pronounced choices is an effective way to overcome procrastination. The choices you make, Fritz suggests, are best made regularly, regardless of how you feel at the moment you make them.

Whether you are angry, anxious, elated, or sad; goofy, dopey, bashful, or sneezy; you are constantly making choices that affect your behavior and performance.

You cannot gain control merely by reacting and responding. Doing that decreases your power to choose. By discerning how you feel and acknowledging your present emotions, you release blocked energy and gain a fuller sense of the present. You have more control over how you choose to feel and act.

> *"Procrastination becomes less likely on tasks that we openly and freely choose to undertake."*
> —STEVE PAVLINA

By continuing to make positive choices, you can preserve and broaden your sense of control. On the following page are a few examples of the choices you can make to vanquish procrastination and ignite the self-starter within.

Note that all the choices are worded to indicate what you want, not what you wish to avoid. ("Gosh, I hope I don't step in a cow patty. . . . ") It's important to keep this distinction clear when formulating your own choices. There is little power in choosing by avoidance, but there is great power in directly addressing what you want.

I choose to:

- Easily get started on the task at hand
- Enjoy my work
- Easily acknowledge my completions each day
- Make steady progress
- Maintain balance and harmony
- Remain organized and in control
- Feel comfortable in the face of uncertainty
- Approach my task with enthusiasm
- Masterfully handle the challenges I face
- Maintain high productivity all day
- Build momentum toward goals
- Form powerful partnerships with coworkers
- Leave work feeling energized
- Make new choices as needed
- Make choices that will actually work for me
- Rely more on myself and less on this book

Remember, you are in control of your progress and how your day unfolds. Choose success!

32 **Allow Time for Reflection** When I travel around the country speaking to organizations, it repeatedly dawns upon me how many people in the audience seem perpetually overwhelmed. The irony is that these people could take breaks throughout their days and weeks, but they don't.

Perhaps the biggest obstacle to consistent productivity is the unwillingness to allow yourself some "time-outs" (like the recesses you used to have in elementary school). Everyone needs a few moments for quiet reflection. Even toddlers benefit from a few minutes in the time-out chair. Couldn't everyone greatly benefit from quiet reflection? Would the tasks and projects you face seem so onerous if you could pause for contemplation?

How would your stress level, your life, your career, and the challenges you face be perceived if you engaged in appropriate, reliable ways to find solace and inner guidance in the here and now, at home, at work, and everywhere in between? I spoke to one group of executives and their spouses, and learned from many spouses that their executive husbands or wives simply do not allow themselves to take breaks. Paradoxically, increasing evidence indicates that executives will be more effective if they pause for an extra minute a couple of times each day. This can be done every morning and afternoon—when returning from the water cooler or restroom, before leaving for lunch, or when returning from lunch. And that's the short list.

> *"Men give me credit for some genius. All the genius I have lies in this: When I have a subject in hand I study it profoundly."*
> —ALEXANDER HAMILTON

Along with quiet reflection, avoid engaging in unnecessary motion and activity. I sometimes conduct a brief exercise with my audiences. I ask audience members to take out their watches and do nothing but stare at them for a solid minute. Few can do it! Today, when we're each continually encountering messages that exalt motion and activity, merely reflecting for a moment, or reading or thinking, doesn't seem to be worthwhile.

Has the following happened to you? Somebody walks by your desk and, horror of horrors, you're reading! Maybe you get a funny look, or you feel guilty because you're not "in motion." You fear that others will think that you're procrastinating! Consider that studies reveal that informed people in executive positions read two to four hours each day. So to be as productive as you need to be, you often act in ways that run counter to what society tells you is "productive activity."

Break out of the mindset imposed by others. When you're at the office, you're not training to run a marathon. Overcome the notion to be in motion. Sometimes the best way to be productive is to sit at your desk doing nothing—at least nothing that looks like anything to people walking by. Reading or looking out the window in contemplation could be the single most important and productive thing you do in a day. It also could be another way you procrastinate in plain sight, but you're a self-starter, so you wouldn't do that—would you?

33 **Reward Yourself** In his book *Bringing Out the Best in People,* Aubrey Daniels, Ph.D., discusses the concept of scheduling a reward following a good performance, known by some as the "Grandma principle." As Grandma would say, you don't get to eat your ice cream until you eat your spinach! If you're facing an unpleasant task, it makes sense to follow that up with something you enjoy doing. In other words, you don't get to do what you enjoy until you do the unpleasant task. And no cheating; you can't secretly feed your vegetables to the dog under the table.

> *"Go confidently in the direction of your dreams. Live the life you have imagined."*
> —Henry David Thoreau

All of psychology holds that behavior that is positively reinforced gets repeated. Think of Pavlov and his pooch. If you reward yourself for accomplishing some of the small steps on the path to procrastinating less, you'll have a greater probability of being successful. Rewards can take various forms. For accomplishing a particular activity, you may decide that calling or e-mailing a friend is a sufficient reward for your accomplishment. For other people, it could be a stroll around the block, a favorite snack, a twenty-minute nap, logging on to that favorite Web site, or a bubble bath.

Some people reward themselves by reading a favorite magazine or book, preparing or eating a favorite dish, watching a show on television, going to a movie, or engaging in some hobby. Others reward themselves by buying something, getting a massage, sitting in the steam room at the gym, or sleeping in late the next morning. Forget the Hummer—you haven't merited it yet.

For some people, simply allowing themselves to daydream is a reward. For others, it is taking no assignments home from work, going a whole weekend without reading, pigging out beyond reason and dignity, playing a musical instrument, or participating in a sport. Even doing a crossword puzzle or taking off early without feeling guilty may be a reward.

Find what tickles your fancy, and use it to gain incentive.

34 **Contract with Yourself** Feature writer and author Dennis Hensley describes what he calls "Advancement by Contract." He suggests carefully selecting three to five major activities in support of some task you want to accomplish and then signing a contract *with yourself* that aids you in completing that task. Hensley says, "A contract takes precedence over everything else. Once under contract, you would have to succeed by a preselected date or else face the consequences of defaulting on the contract."

Make three copies of your contract, and give them to your spouse, a coworker, and a friend who will not question your sanity. Keep the original.

SELF-INITIATED CONTRACT

I, _____ , agree to accomplish each of the following items on or before _____ and hereby do formally contract myself to these purposes. These items are challenging, but reasonable, and I accept them willingly.

A. _____

B. _____

C. _____

Signature: _____ Date: _____

Review your contract when you find yourself becoming distracted by small details or if you think you're not moving in the right direction. (For a more stringent approach along the same theme, see tip #49 on putting money in escrow.)

"Whether you believe you can do a thing or not, you are right."
—HENRY FORD

35 **Produce a Plan** When it comes to starting a task or project, people tend to procrastinate if they lack either a clear starting point or a logical sequence of steps to take. Yet, we all have an inborn capacity to handle such challenges.

A newborn faces the challenge of making sense of sights and sounds. Most of what a baby hears is gobbledygook until the baby can incorporate sounds into the structure of language. Until the baby slowly begins to form words, what he or she utters is nonsense to others. Words such as "mama" (single syllables repeated) "mine," and "the bath was fun but I'd like to get some sleep now" are the baby's first words. Later, the baby tries more complex poly-syllabic words.

The baby eats strained peaches, pears, plums, and other yucky mush. As the baby develops teeth, he can eat more solid and complex foods. The baby plays with simple toys (often brightly colored, washable, inedible, child-safe, and durable) that he hits, bangs, chews on, throws at you, or simply touches.

The baby steadily draws upon basic skills. The baby starts walking by first leaning on the side of a couch or whatever else is handy. In time, the baby takes a step and finally walks across the living room without help. Even then, the baby falls many times, but usually gets up and optimistically begins again.

Concurrently, tackling information, integrating new technology into your work routine, or handling a new project goes more smoothly when you employ the basics: plot a course; take a step at a time; assess where you are every couple of steps; determine that you're on the right path; measure your progress; practice; and then, develop a new routine. Plotting a course need not be a complicated process. For the rank-and-file tasks you might put off, simply sketch out on a piece of paper the five, seven, nine, or however many steps that are required to accomplish the deed. This is a critical first step on the high road to completing the task.

When you plot your course of action, suddenly the task seems easy. You have a path. The path might be hard, but you now have some direction. Okay, you still may need a high-tech compass and full-range radar detector, but at least you no longer have to rely on moss growing on trees or the position of the North Star.

Your written course could entail a few key words or phrases listed in progression—the progression you believe is correct at the outset. Later, your path can be revised as the situation merits. Just as the pilot of an airplane makes constant readjustments during the flight, you may find yourself shifting time lines as you become more aware of the realities of accomplishing your task. Hey, this is not an excuse to let you change your time lines at will. It's simply an acknowledgment that planning to pursue a task and actually pursuing it include different kinds of activities.

If you need help tackling large tasks, a program like Above & Beyond might be just the ticket. As described at *www.1soft.com*, Above & Beyond helps you to "split large projects into definable tasks and generate reports and invoices." Some people, however, believe that they can skip plotting a course altogether because they have "weighed" the steps in their minds. While you may be among the talented few who do not need to map out a course of action, write it down anyway, because it will unburden you mentally in ways you may not have considered. In essence, you decongest your brain. Once your path is "out of your head" and "on the page" you are free to direct your mental energy to completing each particular step, without being nebulously concerned with the entire process.

"The future belongs to those who believe in the beauty of their dreams."
—ELEANOR ROOSEVELT

Many a large task or project has been successfully executed by those with the wherewithal and patience to craft a succinct outline or plan of attack, and the energy and discipline to stick to it.

When mega-novelist John Grisham writes one of his new legal thrillers, he charts a course of action on a dimension most people would never attempt. In brilliant detail, Grisham completes a comprehensive outline sequence for every chapter. His outlines range between sixty and eighty pages! Most people, especially me, are not willing to devote that kind of attention to any project, let alone the *planning* of a project. Grisham has repeatedly used this process to achieve his spectacular success.

When he begins writing the narrative portion of a book, at no point along the trail is he ever lost. He refers to his comprehensive outline—his grand course of action—and knows exactly what to write next. If such a procedure works so marvelously well on enormous projects, think of what a simple plan—not necessarily longer than the length of a Post-it pad—can do for seat-of-the-pants, shoot-from-the-hip you.

36 **Bargain with Yourself** One effective way to defeat the procrastination beast is to cut a deal with someone nearby—yourself. The deal is something I call a "dynamic bargain." A dynamic bargain is an agreement you make with yourself to assess what you've accomplished (and what more you want to accomplish) from time to time throughout the day, adjusting to new conditions as they emerge. A dynamic bargain is a self-reinforcing tool for achieving a desired outcome that you've identified within a certain time frame. Here's the magic phrase to employ: *"What would it take for me to feel good about ending work on time today?"*

> *"Right now is the most important moment in your life."*
> —ROBERT FRITZ

Suppose that on any given day, your answer to the question is to finish three particular items on your desk. Now imagine that your boss drops a work bomb on your desk late in the day and you find yourself preparing for a shrapnel dinner. There's no need to explode; instead, you automatically get to strike a new dynamic bargain with yourself! Given the circumstances, your new bargain may include simply making sufficient headway on the project that's been dropped in your lap or accomplishing two of your previous three tasks and X percent of this new project.

By employing such a question and striking a dynamic bargain with yourself, you avoid what many professionals still confront: dawdling as the end of a time interval approaches (such as before lunch or at the end of the day). Regardless of projects, e-mail, phone calls, or other intrusions into your otherwise perfect world, continually strike a dynamic bargain with yourself so you remain productive and end your day feeling good about what you accomplished.

37 **Sum Up the Costs** Have you ever considered *all* the costs of procrastination, not merely the mental anguish, hand-wringing, and gnashing of teeth? When you are especially stuck getting started on some important task, write the following headings on a piece of paper: mental, monetary, psychic, professional, social. Leave at least an inch and a half between headings.

Now consider the mental costs. You probably know these all too well. They might involve sleepless nights, anxiety, headaches, psychological battles, lions and tigers and bears. Oh my!

What is the actual monetary cost of not getting started on this task? The answer may range from nothing to hundreds or even thousands of dollars, particularly if a career or business opportunity is at stake. And, ohmigosh, what if it's all your money?

The psychic costs may be even greater. What is the cost of regarding yourself as unproductive, lazy, or comatose? It might cause you to avoid other types of challenges because you fear that you will procrastinate to the same degree. You may even allow feelings of worthlessness to affect your relationships.

If you are known as someone who drops the ball or, worse, never even picks it up, peers and associates may not want to work with you. Professionally speaking, the costs can be devastating. Perhaps your proclivity to procrastinate has cost you raises and promotions. What if no one will tell you this?

"The problem is not that there are problems. The problem is expecting otherwise and thinking that having problems is a problem."
—THEODORE RUBIN

From a social standpoint, procrastinating can keep you from meeting new friends, a significant other, and who knows who else. It's like being the smelly kid in class. No one will go near you and you probably won't know why! You may miss out on social opportunities or finding your fifteen minutes of fame because of your inability to take action. Hesitation may prevent you from enjoying the time you have for social activities, because you keep fretting about the tasks you've been putting off. Avoid a seizure, enjoy some leisure.

Sometimes when you add up the costs of not getting started, it can be startling. Procrastination comes with a price tag. The stark realization of its costs may be enough to light a fire under you.

38 **Rest Well and Eat Healthy** Those days when you simply "can't get started" follow a pattern. Yet, you often procrastinate without the slightest clue as to why. Usually such days come when your poor frazzled brain has decided that you need to put a little relaxation back into your life. You need rest when you are tackling a rigorous project. If you don't give yourself the rest you need, or the proper nutrition, your body has a way of seeking revenge on you, and it ain't pretty. As humorist Scott Friedman says, some people think a balanced diet is a cookie in each hand.

"A problem difficult at night is resolved in the morning after the committee of sleep has worked on it."
—JOHN STEINBECK

Some experts believe that getting too little sleep on a consistent basis may undermine your entire being—detrimentally impacting your entire life. Adults need nap time, too! Any illness that you do contract, combined with too little sleep, will be more severe. Your ability to tackle life's challenges will be hampered. Here's a list of indicators showing that you're not getting enough sleep:

- Your eyes arc red, and coworkers keep commenting on your new "demonic" look.
- You're not mentally sharp; you couldn't even cut Scotch tape.
- You avoid tasks that involve adding up numbers.
- You often find yourself daydreaming.
- In situations with others you simply go through the motions.
- You don't want to handle any phone calls if you can help it.
- You watch the clock frequently throughout the day, hoping the time will go by more quickly.
- You doze off before you finish reading this list.

When you rob yourself of the necessary sleep you need on a consistent basis, the recovery period from the day's stresses that proper sleep provides becomes more important than ever. While recovery also comes as a result of being mentally and physically relaxed, getting deep sleep is critical for the challenging tasks you face on a day-in, day-out basis.

Deep rapid eye movement (REM) sleep enables you to more fully engage in conceptual, first-time, and breakthrough thinking. If you have to learn a new routine, new instructions, or new equipment, the amount and quality of REM sleep you get the night before will decidedly impact your abilities and your potential for procrastinating the next day. If your REM pattern is disrupted, even eight hours of sleep may not yield the benefits you need to be effective.

Paradoxically, you're most likely to resist allowing yourself a recovery period—that is, getting a good night's sleep—precisely at that time when you're most in need of it! This explains why you find yourself watching yet another television program or visiting another Web site past the time you know you need to be in bed, when the best thing for you would be to get some zzz's. You pay heavy dues when you stay up to watch the late-night news. No, Leno and Letterman are not considered news.

Worth Knowing

For most people, the time when they are least alert is between 2 A.M. and 5 A.M. Highest alertness is between 9 A.M. and noon, and between 4 P.M. and 8 P.M. Your alertness will vary depending on your own physiology and inclinations, as well as on hours of consecutive duty, hours of work in the preceding week, irregular hours, monotony on the job, timing and duration of naps, environmental lighting, sound, aroma, temperature, cumulative sleep deprivation over the past week, and more. Even talking about sleep deprivation is exhausting!

Hereafter, if you are having trouble starting a task, remember that you may be tired or hungry. Half the time the reason you can't get started on something is because you are fatigued. When you don't have enough sleep and haven't eaten well, even the dinkiest tasks seem more draconian than they actually are. When you're well rested and well nourished, you have the best chance of doing your best work.

39 **Master the Three-to-Five Method** For whatever you're trying to tackle, find some element of it that you can complete quickly and easily, and get an immediate "win." Even if it's an itsy, bitsy, tiny win. For most career professionals, that's a far easier method of getting started than tackling a difficult portion of it first. If you can tackle several small tasks, all the better.

Using a method espoused by time management guru Alan Lakein, ask yourself, "What are three to five things I could do to progress toward the final objective, without actually tackling a project head-on?" Then initiate these "easy entry" activities. Often, they are enough to get your motor running, and head out on the highway.

As an example, suppose you're facing a difficult project. How could you get an easy win right off the bat? Open up the file folder, visually scan the contents, and look for something that's familiar to you. Often, that represents an easy entry point.

Conversely, sometimes simply organizing materials, putting them into smaller file folders, stapling items, bookmarking Web sites or rearranging the order of things represents a good, early win. Now at least you have a better handle on the project, the supporting items are arranged in their order of importance, and the probability that you'll continue on is reasonably assured.

Suppose you've been putting off some task assigned to you, such as moving files into storage. What chance is there of employing the three-to-five method here? After all, you either move the files or not, right? Not exactly.

You could first obtain the huge pushcart you'll need to haul the contents away. You may want to ensure that you have your sleeves rolled up (this is not the time for French cuffs!). It might make sense to sift through the items to survey the scope of work. No use getting started on something when you haven't surveyed the grounds. You might decide to divvy up the documents into quarters and tackle one on Monday morning, one on Monday afternoon, one on Tuesday before midday, and one on Tuesday evening. You might let a coworker know that you want assistance on Monday and Tuesday evening in filling up at least one portfolio each time, as your own energy sags along with your vertebrae.

"Procrastination is the thief of time."
—Edward Young

There . . . you've engaged in five entry activities. Can there be any doubt that you won't proceed as scheduled? Okay, some doubt, but far less than prior to your five entry activities, and you probably don't want that huge pushcart in your office for very long.

40 **Count to Four** To close Part 4, here's a David-sized tip with a Goliath-sized payoff. Suppose you don't want to tackle something right now but know eventually you're going to have to start it. One way to get yourself immersed in it, kind of like dangling your feet in a pool, is to devote four minutes of your attention to the task. At the end of four minutes you may stop. "Once you pop, the fun don't stop!"

What happens to most people when they use this four-minute approach is that they don't want to stop after the fourth minute. Why? Impetus. A body, or a mind for that matter, to keep Descartes happy, tends to keep progressing in the same direction. In science this is known as inertia. If you've been on a project for four minutes, there is no reason why the fifth, sixth, or seventh minute is any more trying.

> *"Heroism consists in hanging on one minute longer."*
> —NORWEGIAN PROVERB

Hereafter, if you are having a hard time getting started on a task, promise yourself that you'll engage in it for *only* four minutes. After four minutes, you have the option of stopping or continuing. Fortunately, many times, once you get in motion, you're more than willing to keep on truckin'.

Take On the Harder Tasks

41 **Stay Fit; Keep It Fun** Have you put off exercising . . . for weeks, months, or even . . . years? You probably already know that the people of industrialized nations around the world, especially the United States, are battling weight problems and obesity unlike any generation before them. Staying fit carries over into many aspects of your work and your life. To start off Part 5, let's examine an innovative way to stop procrastinating when it comes to exercise.

An ultraeffective method to stay fit is to make your workouts learning experiences. I've embarked upon a new approach to stay in shape and become much more knowledgeable than I ever thought I could be. I go to the video store and rent a video series on topics of science, history, geography, and so on. While exercising I am adding to my storehouse of knowledge or understanding of human endeavors. Okay . . . sometimes I'll pop in a Jackie Chan movie.

All of a sudden, when I come home in the evening feeling dead tired from working so hard, instead of procrastinating when it comes to staying fit, I have a viable option before me: watch one of the videos and start exercising. Even if I simply watch it and do stretches, my body, as well as my mind, is getting some benefit, and besides, Jackie Chan can be quite inspiring.

> *"Do not let circumstances control you. You change your circumstance."*
> —JACKIE CHAN

It's not quite the same as reading literature, but a good video may encompass broad expanses of time, scenery, and writing. By exercising at the same time, you can avoid the tendency most people have to eat while they watch television. You'll be a hot tomato instead of a couch potato. Meanwhile, worlds open up, both mentally and physically. If you've been putting off engaging in a regular program of exercise for too long, here is your golden opportunity.

Ready, Willing, and Have Cable

How might this system be put to work for you? With most homes containing two or three television sets, including DVD players, you probably have a television at your disposal. Rent a short video series for openers. Watch it for twenty minutes or so, turn off the DVD, go take a shower, and come back to watch the rest of it. In essence, you've created an exercise and mini learning session on your own.

Suppose you insist that you have absolutely no time—that your spouse, your children, and/or your job slurp up all of your day. Arise and shine an hour earlier and do your viewing before everyone else is up, or do it early in the evening before dinner. Let others in your household know that you are carving out twenty, thirty, or forty minutes, however much time it takes you to do the exercises that you want to do so many times per week.

To get started you will have to identify which videos you actually want to watch. If you can help it, skip the car chase stuff and go for classy material instead. Log on to Netflix, take a trip to your local video store, your local library, or even check out used-book shops that may carry alternative media. Talk to your friends. What do they already own? Swapping video series is a wonderful way to gain hours and hours of great viewing and exercise without paying a dime.

And, if you can't squeeze in even one creampuff exercise session at home, look for ways to get exercise on the job, such as parking in the farthest spot in the garage or parking lot, using the stairs as often as is practical instead of taking the elevator, and taking a five- to ten-minute walk after lunch.

42 **Dive Right In** This is not recommended for everyone, and certainly not every time. Sometimes the only way to get started on a task is to dive into it headlong, cold turkey, not allowing yourself the opportunity to stray. Surprisingly, when you practice the cold-turkey approach to procrastination, it's not nearly as upsetting as it sounds. In fact, it can be a great relief.

If you saw the 1987 movie *Broadcast News* with Holly Hunter and William Hurt, you'll recall the scene in which a party is disrupted so that the staff can get back to the studio to cover late-breaking news. There is no time to lose, and she who hesitates is lost. Hunter's character, Jane Craig, takes command in a cold-turkey situation.

She starts directing virtually everyone in the newsroom, encouraging some, tongue-lashing others, so that the station is able to present a timely, professional, insightful news alert to its viewers. The segment comes off well, and everyone in the station celebrates. If they'd had more time to prepare themselves, the broadcast segment might not have been as compelling (and the movie itself wouldn't have been as good.)

> *"I ain't wasting time no more, 'cause time goes by like hurricanes and faster things."*
> —GREGG ALLMAN

Think of the person who stands on the side of pool in endless turmoil about whether to dive in, jump in, climb down the pool ladder, or sit on the side of the pool and slowly try to get acclimated to the water.

I can barely watch such people. A good shove is what they need. . . . It would only take one second to jump in and another six to eight seconds to get "used to" the water.

My friend Jim Cathcart, a fellow professional speaker, made the decision a few years back to chuck all of his hard-copy slides en masse so that he would be forced to learn presentation software and convert his audio-visuals to newer, more powerful media. Sometimes, you simply have to jump in. When you do, you know down to the marrow in your bones, more often than you might imagine, that you're on the right path. You might even wonder why you spent so much time getting started.

43 **Listen to Yourself** In his book *Emotional Resilience,* author David Viscott, M.D., recounts a startling observation he made in counseling patients. To be of greater service to his clients, and for his own records, he began recording client sessions. Dr. Viscott asked patients to describe their problems and what they thought was holding them back.

When the doctor replayed the tape for patients on subsequent visits, something unpredictable happened. As patients listened to themselves describe their own problems and obstacles to solving them, the tales of woe became insufferable. It seems that the patients' own rationales and excuses for not moving on were too much to bear. They did not want to hear their own feeble, flimsy arguments, which had long been playing over and over again in their minds. Blessed are those who can laugh at themselves, for they shall never ceased to be amused.

Many patients were able to achieve breakthroughs as a result of encountering these tapes of themselves. The hardship of actually doing something about the problem was more palatable than the hardship of having to listen to their own lame excuses.

Similarly, when you find yourself procrastinating, grab a pocket recorder and lay out the task or project as you understand it. Ruminate on the one or many reasons why you cannot begin. Hours or days later, replay your recording. If you are like most people, you will find listening to the tape to be painful. As you hear in your own words the reasons you have given for not getting started, breakthroughs may occur.

"If we don't change, we don't grow. If we don't grow, we aren't really living."
—GAIL SHEEHY

During such a replay, your reasoning may astound you. You may be shocked, disgusted, or simply amused. Some people report that they can't believe they said what they said and worse, can't believe that such empty arguments merited inaction. You will "hear through" your own lame excuses ("bad hair day") and justifications for inaction. You may think, "How could I have let such namby-pamby excuses keep me from taking action?"

44 **Team Up on Your Way to Achievement** In tips #26 and #28 you learned the value of affiliating with others who face the same task as you and of getting help on some tasks from a knowledgeable coworker. For long-term success, seek out a viable partner who can help you get started and stay on course. Both at work and away from it, partners have achieved some pretty remarkable things.

Whether it's:

• Lenin and Trotsky (partners in convoluted political revolution)

- Lennon and McCartney (partners in song for the legendary Beatles)
- Lerner and Loewe (partners in show tunes)
- Leopold and Loeb (partners in crime)
- Lewis and Clark (partners in geographic exploration)
- Lois and Clark (partners in journalism—in comic books!)

. . . teams have been a part of the landscape for as far back as history stretches. Go team, go! The synergy that some teams muster is a marvel to behold. There's something about working in unison that can spur people to rise above their typical performance standards.

So, in considering the potential of successful partnerships, and your own aspirations, whom do you know who could help you?

"Two are better than one; . . . for if they fall, the one will lift up his fellow; But woe to him that is alone when he falleth. And hath not another to lift him up."
—ECCLESIASTES 4:9–10

There's something special about having one other person with whom you collaborate, and it often can bring out the best in both of you. You don't even have to like each other! Richard Rodgers and Oscar Hammerstein of Rodgers and Hammerstein frequently feuded with each other and allegedly did not converse with one another *other than when working*. Lennon and McCartney had their spats along the way in an otherwise brilliant partnership. Even Bert and Ernie have been known to get on each other's nerves, and look how long they've stuck together.

As long as the coworkers respect the talents or contributions of the other, partnerships can go on and on, independent of what type of relationship the individuals have otherwise. It helps especially if you can find someone who has already had to tackle what you currently face. If you like your partner, consider that gravy with your mashed potatoes!

45 **Delegate or Die** Where is it written that you have to handle each and every task or project confronting you? Many readily lend themselves to delegation. It is not necessarily shirking the task to find someone else who can effectively complete a task for you. In your domestic life, you can potentially enroll your children as house serfs, or hire someone. Watch out if you start believing that you alone are the only one who can handle all tasks!

Throughout the course of my career in writing books and speaking to groups, I have employed part-time helpers, mainly college students, who are skilled at copyediting and proofing. Some of these people are brilliant, and they're only twenty years old! They make some money practicing their good grammar, and I don't have to deal with it. Everybody wins! In speeches, when I explain the value of shelling out immigrant wages for others to handle the tasks you'd rather dismiss, someone always asks, "What do I do if money is tight?"

I don't presume that you have trunkloads of cash stashed away somewhere, and I am aware that most people spend more than they have. Granted, the thought of parting with some of your money to hire people to do what you've traditionally done yourself may seem like heresy at first. Consider the act of hiring others a means of vanquishing procrastination on tasks that need to be done, thus freeing up your time for other, possibly more important tasks.

It makes perfect sense to pay a high-school student $15 to mow the lawn if you despise mowing it yourself. You have things to accomplish that can perhaps make you much more money than the $15 you pay somebody to cut the grass or trim the hedges. In the long run, you won't miss the money, and you'll be glad you're no longer mowing the lawn.

If you operate your own business, there are many instances in the course of a day, week, or season where you could benefit by delegating the tasks and responsibilities that inevitably mount up. What could helpers accomplish for you? Take a look:

- Serve routine customer needs
- Make deliveries and pickups
- Route/sort the mail
- Answer requests for information
- Send out mailings of any sort
- Make first-round or lead calls to prospective customers
- Hunt for a product or service you need
- Catalog new information or products
- Proofread or double-check anything written
- Survey customers and assess their needs
- Keep track of necessary data and news sources
- Type mailing lists
- Type anything, for that matter
- Keep things tidy, clean, and in good repair
- Study competitors, their literature, and their products
- Track inventory or arrange displays
- Pick up breakfast or lunch
- Do your laundry (if you're lucky)

If you work for an organization, there are still countless opportunities for relief. At work as well as away from work, you can rely on others to complete the tasks you don't enjoy.

If the whole project can't be delegated, is there a portion of it that you can delegate? Particularly the part you don't like to do or aren't good at doing? Let's face it, there are some tasks that you're not going to do well, no matter how hard you try, how many lessons you take, and how long you practice. Let it go!

> *"The secret of success lies not in doing your own work but in recognizing the right person to do it."*
> —ANDREW CARNEGIE

Some people will never be good at playing the piano, some will never be good at computer programming, and some people will never be good at creative writing. This is simply human nature. If you want to "nurture your nature," as author Jim Cathcart says in his book *The Acorn Principle,* capitalize on your strengths and shore up your weaknesses by getting help.

This is your newfound mission, and it makes sense to accept it: Identify all those essential but bothersome tasks you've been putting off, and hire someone else to handle the unpalatable. Who knows? Some people might actually like proofreading.

46 Do One Thing at a Time Somehow juggling tasks (see tip #56 on multitasking) has gained a strong foothold in how we work and live. Man, how in the world did this happen? In continually switching, you can end up playing a subtle game of procrastination with yourself wherein you're actually avoiding the one key task among the many that need to be finished. You can't fool me; I know what you're up to.

The single best way, however, to cope with a number of different projects is to begin working on one thing until its completion, then go on to the next project, then the next, until you are finished.

What occurs when you jump between different projects? It may feel dynamic—after all, you're exerting lots of energy. You almost feel like shouting, "Look at me!" Yet there's a loss of productivity. You and a friend can test this easily at your desk or table. Decide on any three minor tasks in which the two of you can engage simultaneously. For example, one task could be stacking pennies, another could be drawing fifteen stars on a blank sheet of paper, and yet another could be linking paper clips together. You each have the same number of items.

"Until you value yourself, you won't value your time. Until you value your time, you will not do anything with it."
—M. Scott Peck

You and your friend both engage in these tasks. You stack a few pennies at a time, make a few stars on a blank piece of paper, and link some paper clips, indiscriminately alternating among the three tasks.

Meanwhile, on the other side of the table, your friend stacks an equal number of pennies to completion—until he has no more. Then he turns to making stars on a page until he reaches fifteen. Finally he turns to linking paper clips, and he finishes linking all of them.

Who do you think will not only finish faster and more easily but be in better shape mentally and emotionally? Without question, your friend. Why? Lucky day? No. He was able to focus on the task at hand, take it to completion, then turn to the next one, while you were bouncing back and forth among activities. You also may have been more prone to errors, such as knocking over one of your stacks of pennies, but that might just be because you're clumsy, which is another issue all together.

Although you handled the situation well and were quite adept at it, you simply couldn't keep pace. The quality of your work suffered, too. Perhaps your work was not as precise, or the fifteen stars you drew on the page left much to be desired in terms of artistic merit, or whatever.

When you multiply what happens in a simple test such as this by what happens all day and all year long when you flip-flop between activities, it's easy to understand why you're not getting the most out of the time you put in. Mentally switching from task to task is not as productive as staying on one job until completion. Give yourself the benefit of working on one thing at a time.

If staying on task seems onerous, periodically assessing your progress can help.

One of the all-time sweetest things is hearing your name called when you're on the airline wait list. You step onboard and are ready to be whisked home. Most passengers don't know this, but the typical commercial airline flight is off-course the majority of the time. The pilot takes off and assumes a course heading. Then, because of prevailing winds and a host of other factors, the pilot finds himself off course by a half a degree. He adjusts and gets back on course. A few minutes later, he might be off a couple of degrees in the other direction.

For the duration of the trip, the plane veers this way and that off the path of the desired course. Through enhanced navigational systems and the work of the pilot, the plane continually readjusts and gets back on course. Eventually, as the plane is about to land and course settings become critical, all attention is focused on assuring a safe landing. If the captain were to announce over the intercom every little deviation in course, the passengers would be nervous wrecks, more than some already are. They would lose confidence in that pilot, the crew, and that airline in particular.

If they heard the same type of reports on the next plane they boarded, they might lose confidence in that airline as well. Yet, continual monitoring and adjustments during flights are the norm, not the exception.

For the multitude of tasks you face, veering off course on one or many of them is an everyday phenomenon. That is why switching between projects is risky. Being just a few percentage points off in the early phases of a project can yield dramatic negative results later. How do you counteract this? Stay focused on the task at hand and periodically monitor your overall progress, and keep your seat locked in the full, upright position.

47 **Apply the Heavy Half Mentality** Adopting the heavy half mentality works particularly well for highly challenging tasks or projects. On a long and grueling trip, if you were only to make one stop, it might be wise to make it somewhere past halfway. If you stop someplace before halfway, getting started again could be worse than breaking up a catfight. You mentally compute how much time it took you to reach where you are and how much time is left, and the figures don't look good!

When you travel at least 55 percent, 60 percent, or 65 percent of the way toward completing your journey and then pause to consider that you are closer to your destination than to your point of origin, it's somewhat easier to continue. I can personally attest to this—I invented the approach!

In the early 1970s I used to drive Mr. Mott's Cadillac from West Hartford, Connecticut, down to Miami Beach, Florida. Mr. Mott—I never knew his first name and never dared to ask— owned Mott's Supermarkets and ultimately branched out to other products, including Mott's Apple Juice. When he needed his car for business in Florida, he would pay responsible college students to make that twenty-seven-hour drive for him. He would then fly down and meet the students, pay them an agreed-upon fee, and give them a one-way airline ticket back.

My strategy in driving Mr. Mott's car was to never stop to sleep at the halfway point. It would be too grueling to know that the next day, I would have to drive as long as I already did. Moreover, I didn't want to travel only a little past halfway either. I made it my business to go two-thirds of the way—eighteen hours before stopping for the night.

Leaving at 5 or 6 A.M. and taking breaks only to pump gas and visit the restroom, I proceeded on until 12 or 1 in the morning. With a good eighteen hours under my belt, the combination of a good night's sleep and the knowledge that there were only nine more hours to go always left me feeling satisfied and eager to finish the final leg of my journey.

You can use the heavy half approach when writing a report, making a long presentation, tackling a household project, or enduring any other challenging activity or event. It probably makes sense not to reveal your strategy except when giving a presentation. In that case, let your audience in on this strategy so that they won't become fidgety as you approach and pass the halfway point in your session.

"Slow and steady wins the race."
—AESOP

Once you have used the heavy half approach in various settings, you realize that you can apply it to almost everything. For example, if there is a big expense from the Home Shopping Network you have to pay and you would rather make it in two installments, don't make the installments equal. Pay a little more on the first installment so that you can pay a little less on the second one.

When you engage in any task, go beyond halfway before taking a "midway" pause. By taking care of the heavy half first, and acknowledging this completion, you leave yourself far more energized to complete the shorter, lighter second half. You arrive *more* than alive.

Yes, it takes some discipline and rigor to proceed past halfway and complete the heavy half, but once you do, you will find the payoff to be so rewarding you may never stop halfway again! Although, if you're driving and need to stop halfway to use the restroom, I won't think poorly of you.

48 **Employ the Bigger and Badder Method** Here is a system of tradeoffs that I've used over the years. You can harness your procrastination to create energy for handling the tasks before you. Let's say you've got Project A. It's big, it's bad, it's scary, and you've been putting it off for weeks. "I came, I saw, I declined." All of a sudden Project B comes along, and B is worse! Now, you've got a big incentive to make B what you're procrastinating about and initiate A. I do this all the time, and I've done it for years.

Suppose your income taxes are due, and you have been putting off preparing and filing the forms. Perhaps you look around the room for every other thing that you can take care of to make yourself feel as if you are staying productive (you can only vacuum the couch so many times). Then, suppose some other major task arises that is worse than doing your taxes (and there aren't many like that—delousing your pet sloth, maybe!).

Suddenly, completing your taxes doesn't seem so big or so bad. Compared to whatever else you may be facing, if completing your taxes represents the lesser of two evils, and you're able to start on the taxes promptly, you've appropriately employed the bigger and badder method of overcoming procrastination! Actually, almost everybody employs this technique unconsciously at one time or another.

Use the psychic energy that surrounds you when a new project comes on the horizon and trade off what it is you're procrastinating as a way to propel you at least to get on to that second one. When that second one is complete and the first one is still there, that may now become the biggest and baddest—or there may be a new task that comes along. If you can continue to recognize bigger and badder tasks on the horizon, whatever ominous task you are currently facing will seem much more palatable.

"To avoid criticism, do nothing, say nothing, and be nothing."
—ELBERT HUBBARD

Some experts criticize substituting one activity for another. If you take on onerous Project B because you would rather not proceed with more onerous Project A, there is widespread agreement that you're procrastinating. My view is that if Project B has timely value, you will be much better off once it's completed. You can start on A relatively soon thereafter, thus having successfully applied a form of time-shifting.

Later, if something else comes along that is "worse" than A, you again benefit from the bigger and badder assignment because it will make tackling A seem a lot easier than it previously had seemed.

49 **Establish an Escrow** At one time or another, you have probably come across the strategy of placing a significant sum, say $500, in escrow until you complete a given project that you have been putting off. Within some prescribed amount of time, if you don't complete the project you forfeit the sum; whoever was holding it for you retains it.

To safeguard the disbursement of such funds if you fail to complete the agreed-upon task, be sure that the person holding the sum is someone you like and someone you would like to see receive the money. Conversely, to ensure that you won't procrastinate, choose an escrow holder whom you would not like to have winning your money, such as someone at work who is trustworthy but is not otherwise one of your favorite people. Now you have the added incentive of not only losing the money but having it go out the door not to family and friends but into the hands of some Marxist fascist.

Money is the root of all wealth. Putting money in escrow is a powerful technique for those tortured souls who have unsuccessfully battled procrastination. The key to effectiveness is ensuring that the sum is significant to you. If losing $500 means nothing to you (and if that's true, lunch is on you this week), pick a larger sum for which you would experience pain and/or gnashing of teeth.

"Time is money."
—BENJAMIN FRANKLIN

You want to put enough money into escrow so that relinquishing it can have significant long-term ramifications. For many people, losing a sizable sum held in escrow makes a deep impact. Thereafter, if you have the guts to put a second sum in escrow, you are more likely to accomplish the agreed-upon task. If you lose this second sum as well, then abandon this strategy before you go bankrupt; it is simply not for you!

50 **Seek Counseling** If you have been putting off something so intently that you are disturbing your own professional or domestic tranquility, it may be time to seek help from a professional counselor. I do not advocate going to a counselor at the drop of a hat. Certainly friends, associates, relatives, supervisors, and mentors may assist you in particular situations.

"Forget regret, or life is yours to miss."
—JONATHAN LARSON

When the situation becomes too difficult to bear, go to someone who has been educated and professionally trained to help with such types of issues, and I don't mean watching Dr. Phil. These professionals may include psychiatrists, psychologists, therapists, and other counselors.

- *Psychiatry* is the field of medicine that specializes in prescribing medications for psychological disorders. This requires a medical degree and specialized training in the effects of certain medications. Psychiatrists are doctors who have completed a residency in psychiatry.
- *Psychoanalysis* is an approach to therapy, human nature, and personality theory that emphasizes the role of unconscious motivation in conscious behavior. By being aware of the patient's verbal and nonverbal communications, psychoanalysts can offer interpretations.
- *Therapy* refers to the treatment and care of someone to combat disease, injury, or mental disorder. Probably everyone could use a little therapy at one time or another.
- *Psychotherapy* is the use of psychological methods to treat abnormal or disordered behavior. It is needed for individu-

als suffering from pronounced psychopathologies, such as schizophrenia and severe depression. Treatment strategies often include medication, and sometimes hospitalization.

- *Family therapy* seeks to identify and correct disruptive and unhealthy patterns characterized by demands and expectations that some family members have for others.
- *Counseling* involves working with a variety of individuals and their everyday problems in individual, family, or group settings.
- *Clinical psychology* is the largest subdiscipline of psychology. Clinical psychologists work in hospitals, clinics, and private practice, focusing on the diagnosis and treatment of learning and emotional problems.
- *Cognitive therapy* refers to the study of thinking, concept formation, and problem solving. This therapy emphasizes changing how the client thinks.

The key concern in working with any type of counseling professional is not to let the reason for your initial appointment expand into a long-term series of expensive and time-consuming sessions, unless, of course, you feel the need to go down that path. Sometimes counselors knowingly or unknowingly hook you on a variety of issues; you may find yourself on the lifetime session plan. If you want to tackle problems beyond procrastination, it's your call.

51 **Take Baby Steps** Many people lament that organizing will take too much time. If you think organizing takes too much time, consider how much time disorganization has cost you. Others, less brilliant, say, "I don't see any value in organizing." What they fail to consider is that most aspects of their lives are already organized and now they are simply going to broaden these procedures to a greater extent. The information onslaught is only going to get worse. If you face the future with poor organizational skills, it's like wading waist-high in, shall we say, unpleasantly aromatic organic waste material. Remaining organized is part of the antidote to living in a society overloaded with information.

When you employ a "divide and conquer" mindset, you have a decent chance of staying productive. Some people erroneously maintain an "all or nothing" attitude. For some, that means if they can't begin and finish a task in one sitting, there's no point in getting started, right? "Bollshoi," as they say in Moscow. Rather than trying to tackle, say, a whole file cabinet or all of your desk drawers at once, pick a reasonable goal of organizing only the first half of one drawer this week.

In subsequent weeks tackle the other portions. Regard each half-drawer as a distinct task. In a matter of weeks the job will be done, and you will feel good about it; "weeks" is a lot sooner than never.

"Make hay while the sun shines."
—ENGLISH PROVERB

Remember, the principle is to divide and conquer. Only handle one-half of one drawer at a time.

Suppose you have several tasks before you, each of which would only take five to ten minutes to complete. Any one of these tasks would be no big deal to tackle. The mere thought of handling all of them, however, becomes semi-daunting. As the list of things you need to take care of grows, and you feel yourself getting somewhat behind, they all start to loom even larger! Once again, take bite-size, chewable steps. Don't wolf down your food; the indigestion isn't worth it.

Choose to tackle only two of them for now, if that feels comfortable. When you tackle a ten-minute job, for example, and gain the satisfaction of having it all done, you have more energy, focus, and direction to take on another ten-minute job. That means you may want to finish a third job, and if you have the impetus, there's no better time. It's a natural upper!

52 **Cover the Clock** Most people, more often than we care to admit, don't need to wear a watch. There are all manner of clocks and timepieces surrounding us. If you've got an appointment or if it's important for you to be someplace at a particular time, sure, wear a watch if it's convenient. To stay focused on a project, however, it may be prudent to take off your watch and hide the clock. Don't worry, time will still be there when you put the watch back on.

> *"I go at what I am about as if there was nothing else in the world for the time being."*
> —Charles Kingsley

What happens when you don't wear a watch? You have a better chance of operating at your natural rhythm, which is a far more productive mode than when you monitor yourself based on a clock.

The typical employee comes to work and continually notices what time it is. The clock says 10:15, so that means it's time for coffee, or as I call it, *brown death in a cup*. If you don't look at the clock, you might not get coffee because you might not feel like it at that time. If you don't know what time it is, you respond based on what your body says, not what the clock says. Physiologically speaking, your body will give you the cues you need at precisely the right moment.

When you start a task, such as filling out some form, in view of the clock, it's easy to begin to regard the task as ominous. Yet, if you hide the clock, start working on that form, and return to the world of clocks only when you're finished, you may be stunned to see how little time has passed. A small smile will appear on your face. Do you know that you spend 1/67th of your life looking at a watch or clock? Okay, 1/68th . . .

We've all experienced this phenomenon at one time or another. Time seems to slow down when you are highly focused and not conscious of the time passing. You act at your own internal pace. Away from the clock, big tasks aren't quite as big as they may have loomed in your mind.

So, when possible, avoid wearing a watch or looking at the clock, and give yourself the opportunity to maintain your focus and attention, while establishing your own rhythm. Staring at the clock won't make your lunch break come any faster.

53 **Assess the Effects on Others** Have you ever considered the anxiety and trepidations of others whose work may be affected by your progress on a given task or project? Or is it always all about *you*? Let's not be selfish now. Some enchanted reasoning makes it easier to stay on track when you're able to relate your responsibilities to the larger question of how it contributes to the progress of your team, division, department, organization, or society in general (see tip #4). Conversely, procrastination rears its ugly head when it knows you're working alone, disconnected from others, or unclear about why your work matters.

Individuals cognizant of their impact on others can be heard to say, "I can't afford to be sick; people are counting on me." What this actually means is the speaker recognizes that personal trials and tribulations pale in comparison to the larger problems that can result from succumbing to them.

"Those who stand for nothing fall for anything."
—ALEXANDER HAMILTON

The old axiom "No man is an island" (edited for today to "no person is an island") certainly rings true in your case. Whether or not you have previously acknowledged it, others *are* counting on you to one degree or another. The more vividly you picture or understand who they are and why they need you to pull through, the lower your propensity to procrastinate.

54 **Make Sure Someone Is Expecting Your Work** Here is a quiz question: Why are the phones quiet on October 15 each year? Legions of people file for extensions for their personal income tax returns. Normally, April 15 is the day of anxiety for much of the American public. However, with the ability to file for a six-month automatic extension, millions of people simply shift their anxiety to October. Whether it's paying your taxes or attempting to accomplish almost anything else, given the opportunity to push back the time line—procrastinate—many people will take that opportunity and walk with it. Alternatively, when a completion time is ironclad, the do-it-or-else variety, and somebody (such as the tax collector!) is waiting for you, you tend to get the task done. A strong reason you might finish a task at work is that

. . . drum roll, please . . . you have a boss with a bullhorn in one hand and a whip in the other who awaits your completed work.

"In order that people may be happy in their work, these three things are needed. They must be fit for it, they must not do too much of it, and they must have a sense of success in it."
—JOHN RUSKIN

Even if you don't have a boss for your endeavor, you can pretend that you do. Especially for those times when no matter how hard you try, you still can't get started on a task, ask friends for help. "Friends don't let friends drive naked." If somebody awaits your results, or merely your progress, you significantly increase your ability to start and complete the task at hand.

Beseech a friend to check the task after it's completed, and bid him or her to give you a deadline. While you don't necessarily want to treat personal tasks like assignments, having to report on your progress to someone (it's not just for third graders anymore) will increase your odds of starting and finishing a job in a timely manner.

55 **Grasp the Power of Deadlines** Related to the previous tip, while having someone awaiting your progress can be used to great advantage, don't make the mistake of incurring unnecessary stress by misunderstanding how to best employ deadlines. People often fool themselves by thinking, "I work better under pressure so I don't need to do this now." Statements like these give fuel to procrastination and raise anxiety levels needlessly. Do you want to have to choose between an aneurysm and an ulcer? Hmm, let me think . . .

Let's view deadlines in a way that is productive.

First, unquestionably, most people dread having to work under a deadline. Many people loathe the notorious term itself! "Deadline," a line after which you're dead? Yet, deadlines can serve worthwhile and noble purposes. They enable us to marshal our resources toward accomplishing what might not otherwise ever get done.

Few people enjoy facing a continual trickle of unanticipated, stressful deadlines. With deadlines for which you have fair warning, however, you have options for maintaining control. Suppose that every Thursday you need to submit a report, or every day by noon you have to accomplish a particular task. If you want to keep your job, thrive in the position, and look forward to advancement, you turn in that report on Thursday and you accomplish that task by noon.

You may resent having to handle such responsibility, but resentment mixed with rage, ferocious anger, and homicidal fantasies are the wrong approach. Deadlines can predictably help you to be profitable and competitive, and even be more energetic, vibrant, and alert.

"Seize the day, put no trust in tomorrow."
—Horace

Consider those individuals looking forward to retirement. Does quitting the race create lasting space? The big day comes and is met with joy and celebration. A few months or even weeks later, many retirees find themselves going stir-crazy. As much as they sought retirement, they find that without people to report to, projects to submit, and deadlines to meet, the days can seem like an endless skein.

The human body functions best with established routines such as sleeping the same number of hours each night, eating at certain times, and exercising sufficiently throughout the week. The retiree who faces too few challenges may unknowingly contribute to his or her mental and physical decline. Their former colleagues who are still "in the harness," working at some trade or craft, self-employed or not, for profit or not, can benefit by operating their physical and mental systems at a healthier gear. Deadlines represent an ever-present opportunity to:

1. Realize achievements that might not otherwise come to pass
2. Keep one's bodily systems at optimal capacity
3. Establish or maintain routines that ultimately prove to be positive

If you happen to need assistance when it comes to deadlines, you can download Task Management Software from MyLife Organized (*www.mylifeorganized.net*). This software is designed to help you stay on top of your busy schedule. In a Windows or Pocket PC version, it will generate a to-do list with the steps necessary to complete your goals. As described at *www.mylife organized.net*, "This list of next actions will be sorted in order of priority to keep you focused on the most important tasks." Also, VIP Software at *www.vip-qualitysoft.com/time_management/ procrastination* will notify you by e-mail, phone, or pop-up when a deadline is approaching. The program also boasts the capability to "help you to estimate time required and difficulty of different tasks more realistically."

A wise employee once told me that most people in his organization regarded deadlines as a ball and chain, shackling them to the floor and restricting their movement. His great advantage over his coworkers was recognizing the value of deadlines. Without them, he said, he would have accomplished less than half of what he did accomplish. He understood that routine deadlines convey benefits, and even the nonroutine, drastic, one-of-a-kind deadlines often convey an array of benefits to those who are astute enough to comprehend and work toward meeting them. The gems are buried, not lying on the surface!

Just as you can reframe a task or project and see it in a different light (see tip #3) you can reframe the notion of deadlines—what they mean to you, how you benefit from them, and how you can use them to your advantage.

56 **Annihilate Multitasking** Despite the advantages of working on one thing at time (see tip #46), we all tend to multitask today, perhaps more than we care to admit. At home, we surf the Web while we watch television. At home and at work, we eat while we read. At our desks, we doodle the same type of doodle that we always doodle while we talk on the phone. Usually, there is no real harm in multitasking. As long as you are not driving a car and speaking on a cell phone or operating heavy power equipment under the influence of medication, you are probably okay.

It makes no sense, however, to double up on activities at those times when compromising your attention is risky. You don't want to put on your makeup or shave, as so many people are starting to do, while driving to work in the mornings. Sorry ladies and gents, the clown and the "oh-my-face-got-tangled-in-barbed-wire" looks are not "in" this season. Stay out of my lane, please. Driving requires what researchers call your *sharp attention*. Putting on makeup or shaving also requires such precise attention. You cannot offer your sharp attention at the same time to two different activities that each require it.

If you read at the kitchen table while you eat, you don't taste and enjoy your food to the degree that you could, and you don't absorb what you're reading with your usual retention rate. Nevertheless, you're not going to bounce off a highway guardrail if you eat while you read, so if this is one of your pleasures, keep at it (just don't ruin any good books!).

At work, many people fall into the trap of routinely doubling up on activities in the quest to get more done. However, doubling up seldom carries the benefits that they initially sought.

From the standpoint of effectively initiating a task or project, multitasking is not a great idea or even a good one. You want to give your full and undivided attention to the task at hand. "Full and undivided attention," what a concept! That way you have the best chance of doing a good job, staying focused, and finishing in optimal time.

> *"For him who has no concentration, there is no tranquility."*
> —THE BHAGAVAD GITA

Some people claim that they perform certain tasks better when they have soft music in the background. Perhaps. Some people say if they have some minor distraction (see tip #18 about distractions) it helps them tackle an otherwise challenging project. Okay, I will relent on that one. Be wary, however, if you think you're going to juggle four or five projects, especially if one of them represents something out of the ordinary. It's easier to juggle four tennis balls than three tennis balls and a banana.

If you fall into the trap of believing that you can handle several things at once, the odds are that you will better handle those things that are comfortable, familiar, and easy for you. This is hardly the prescription for rising in your career. Meanwhile you will tend to procrastinate on those tasks that are uncomfortable, not familiar, and more complex for you. Hence, you still have the hard tasks to take care of, and the potential for procrastination grows. You'll constantly be bumping up against work deadlines, making excuses, and overtaxing everyone around you, as well as yourself.

If you eliminate multitasking, your ability to vanquish procrastination will rise dramatically. Your ability to get things done, on time, will improve. People will want to work with you. You can frequently leave at the end of the day with a clear sense of accomplishment.

57 **Post Your Problem** Here's a procrastination-blasting technique that requires only a few minutes to set up and works well for many people. It costs about a dime. When you've been postponing a project, such as cleaning out your desk, write the four words "Clean Out the Desk" on the pages of several Post-it pads and place them throughout your "world."

You might attach one to the file cabinet, for example, and others to the inside of your office door, the dashboard of your car, the side of your bookcase, in your appointment book, and even on the desk door itself. These not-so-subtle reminders begin to filter into your subconscious mind.

Post numerous reminders so that as you go about your day, you can't help but encounter them. You never know which encounter with one of your reminder messages will serve as the final catalyst to prompt you to get started.

The strategy works as well in your domestic life. A friend of mine needed to clean the coils on the back of her refrigerator. So, she posted a note on the refrigerator door. After several days of seeing the note, she decided to temporarily put it on top of the refrigerator. As you might guess, weeks passed without her handling the task. One unassuming day, while dusting the refrigerator top, she encountered the note.

Recognizing that she had put off the task of cleaning the coils for weeks, she reposted the note on the front door of the refrigerator. Sure enough, two days later, she tackled and completed the job. As often happens, the task required less time than she had long contemplated, actually eight minutes. Then, she happily chucked the note.

"Nothing in this world can take the place of persistence."
—CALVIN COOLIDGE

Posting your challenges, big and small, is effective for overcoming procrastination because repeatedly encountering such messages off-guard eventually has its effect. Hence, to make the strategy work for you, do not hide or remove the messages until you complete the task. "Out of sight" of the message equates to "out of mind," and you're not likely to proceed. "In sight" here equals "in mind," and you're far more likely to get the task done.

58 **Decrease Downtime** Can you recall what it was like when you were studying for a test in college? Gosh, it was that long ago? You may have studied alone or with a friend. Perhaps you went to the library or the local coffee hangout. Were you oh-so-lenient with yourself in your study habits? Did you study, or did you watch the parade of passersby?

In my college days, back in the time of troglodytes, it was customary for students to study for fifty minutes and then take a "ten-minute" break—often it stretched beyond ten minutes—and then begin again. Today, a break to check e-mail or chat often leads to an hour of catching up on the latest Britney Spears antics on You-Tube. Nothing is wrong with scheduling break time. A fifty-minute period of concentration followed by, say, a ten-minute period of rest seems practical. Problems occur when break time extends past the allotted time interval and ends up hampering your productivity. By scheduling breaks too frequently, you also may disrupt your productivity and give rise to bouts of procrastination, because you risk not returning to the task at hand and having the break turn into a semi-permanent state.

Consider the situation where someone is studying and does not notice the clock. He or she is making great strides, ingesting and learning the new material. Perhaps this session extends for sixty-five or seventy-five minutes. Lo and behold, the person feels like taking a break. When you take a break upon feeling the need to do so, and not when the clock says so, your productivity often rises because you allow yourself to "stay on a roll." As you learned in tip #52, working based on your own internal rhythms invariably is fulfilling and productive.

Minimizing break time is useful when you're ready to tackle a series of small tasks that you have been putting off. Suppose you have five three- to five-minute tasks confronting you. You decide to give yourself two minutes between each task. The plan seems fairly reasonable on paper, but . . . what if you don't need two minutes between each task? With one task, the "buzz" of your completion will prompt you to start the next task. You may find that a better sequence is to complete three tasks, then give yourself a four-minute break, then complete the final two tasks.

Too much break time invites deviating from intended goals. Besides, most people don't fastidiously ensure that their breaks last only as long as planned. Who knows where the time goes?

When you're able to muster the resolve to handle tasks that you've been putting off, acknowledging the importance of having some breaks lets your *energy level* be your guide. When you are on the proverbial "roll," forgo any planned breaks, recognizing that while it was astute to schedule them, it is more prudent to stay on the roll. You will know instinctively when to pause and, if you are honest with yourself, when to get back to work.

> *"Success seems to be largely a matter of hanging on after others have let go."*
> —WILLIAM FEATHER

Hereafter, to ensure that you complete more of what you want or need to accomplish, carefully safeguard, nurture, and support your propensity to stay on a roll. Keep procrastination at bay and override your earlier plans, however well founded.

59 **Manage Your Life One Day at a Time** In 1913, Yale commencement speaker William Osler charged his listeners to "live in day-tight compartments." By this, he meant accomplish today's work today, and tend to tomorrow's affairs tomorrow. Get good rest, and the next day proceed in the same way. A "day unit" is a convenient measure for charting progress and becoming an effective self-starter. When you work in day units, particularly on a large project, even the most beastly, gawd-awful task seems tamable. How does the day unit work? First consider that:

- Columbus first crossed the Atlantic Ocean in seventy-one days.
- Operation Desert Storm took forty-six days.
- The U.S. Declaration of Independence, from draft to adoption, took twenty-four days to complete. (And all without word-processing software.)
- The 2004 Summer Olympics lasted seventeen days, if you don't count the runners passing the torch.

For large goals, think in day units. That means for nonemergency, noncrunch situations, plan for six hours of concentrated, focused work within a calendar day. Why six hours? With concentrated focus, working six hours is plenty (and most workers rarely average six hours of daily *concentrated* focus on any job). Leave yourself the other two hours for administration, correspondence, and food and bathroom breaks.

"The best thing about the future is that it comes only one day at a time."
—ABRAHAM LINCOLN

Estimate how many day units you'll need to complete a large project. Factor in the weekends, holidays, and other downtime. The figure you derive will be a manageable, meaningful guideline by which your quest can be approached. Many project management software programs enable you to monitor your progress or make adjustments when unforeseen developments arise. If you fall behind on your project you can readjust accordingly. In the rare, fortunate, pinch-me state of getting ahead on the project, you can allocate resources more judiciously than you did initially.

Procrastination is more likely to occur on projects with a long duration: dozens of hours, weeks, or even months. If considerable effort brings you only slightly closer to the project's completion, it may be difficult to see how activities on any given day contribute to long-term progress. To combat the tendency to procrastinate on endless, infinite projects, some people find it worthwhile to devote a fixed time or amount of each day to work on the project. Some devote a minimum of time each day. Some throw up their hands.

One man wanted to be a movie scriptwriter but didn't know how he would make the transition from his job as a foreman in a manufacturing plant. It would have been easy for him to do nothing! He chose to initiate a three-year goal of leaving his job to become a full-time scriptwriter. During the interim, he established a daily goal of spending a minimum of fifteen minutes working on scripts. Some evenings he is able to get two or three pages completed. Other evenings, he is only able to go as far as a paragraph. He also attends scriptwriting seminars and workshops, reads articles and books on the topic, and even attends meetings of a scriptwriters association.

A year and a half into his program, he still checks in daily at the manufacturing plant and still draws 100 percent of his pay as a foreman. Yet, he is enthusiastic about the progress he's making and solidifying his chances for making his living as a movie scriptwriter. Now that's dedication!

60 **Ignore Your Age** Whether you're twenty or sixty years old, or somewhere in between, anytime is a good time to get started on what you seek to accomplish.

> *"How old would you be if you didn't know how old you were?"*
> —SATCHEL PAIGE

Marlee Matlin won the Academy Award for Best Actress at age twenty-one; the late Jessica Tandy won it at age eighty. James Michener didn't write his first novel until age forty-two, the age at which Elvis departed this earth (maybe). Michener then produced one bestseller after another until his death at age ninety. Some people take up marathon running in their fifties; some people begin running in their sixties. Some people's grandmothers could run circles around them, and I don't mean while using an electric wheelchair.

Become comfortable with your current age, and recognize the vast potential you have with all your remaining years. Alyce Cornyn-Selby, a prolific author and speaker from Portland, Oregon, uses two powerful key phrases with her audiences that seem well suited for blasting through the procrastination that sometimes accompanies big projects and lifelong aspirations:

"I have now come to the end of my life and I'm disappointed that I didn't _____."

How did you finish that sentence? Whatever came up first is probably something you want to do right away. No use putting it off any longer, because it bubbled up to the surface immediately.

"I have now come to the end of my life and I'm glad that I _____."

What did you come up with this time? Was it the same issue that you addressed in the first statement? Was it something you've already accomplished? When you begin to look at the opportunities that await and those you can create, procrastination becomes far less of an issue.

It's never too late to start something, especially in the entrepreneurial world. Senior entrepreneurs appear to have the same skills and characteristics that drive younger entrepreneurs: compelling vision, a flair for building, perseverance, positive self-regard, energy, and a passion to succeed. All right, the energy level may not be what it was at twenty-two, but the rest still holds true! Energy is overrated—it's the life experience that gets you ahead! So, don't be afraid to start something new or different at any stage of life; chances are good that it's not too late to succeed.

Summary

Nobody likes procrastination—the act of putting off something until a later time, either by not starting a task or not finishing one you've started. Whenever you let progress on lower-level tasks or projects stand in the way of accomplishing higher-level tasks or projects, you are procrastinating.

When you identify some of the reasons behind procrastination, you have a better chance of getting past them and getting started than you would if you didn't articulate the issues to yourself. So here's the complex solution: Start articulating.

> *"In the depths of winter I finally learned there was in me an invincible summer."*
> —ALBERT CAMUS

At any given time, for any given task, if you have trouble getting started, you now have a variety of techniques to draw upon to get you over the hurdle. Of course, not all techniques work for all people, and no technique will necessarily work for any individual all the time. Try one or another, or another, until you successfully get rolling.

People are more likely to delay taking action when they perceive that something is difficult, unpleasant, or represents a tough choice. Any surprise there? Much of what you may need to undertake to achieve a desired outcome may not please you while you're doing it. True and lasting accomplishments require high costs in terms of hours, energy, and commitment. Unpleasant tasks don't tend to get any more pleasant with the passage of time. So, if you have to do something, you might as well take care of it now.

Sometimes it is understandable and even desirable to do something else other than the task you had originally set out to accomplish, such as when short-term, high-priority tasks or opportunities arise. This does not mean you have a blank check to do whatever you want.

In general, the most successful people in your industry or profession are confident, action-oriented individuals with clear priorities and supporting goals. They know they can't remain productive if they continually meander and don't make the effort to determine what represents their next best move.

Many people believe that if they could only initiate tasks at the "right time," then it would be easier to begin and complete them. For most tasks, there is no opportune moment or "perfect" time, so get over it. True professionals proceed onward independent of their emotions and feelings. They don't wait until they are in the mood.

Other folks think that they need reams of data before making a decision to go ahead or take action. Yet, more data does not necessarily produce a better answer. Don't let data overload contribute to procrastination. Wanting to start on a project is different from deciding to.

One of the biggest obstacles to consistent productivity is the unwillingness to allow yourself some "time-outs." Everyone needs a few moments for quiet reflection. For some, it will be the first time. Looking out the window in contemplation could be the single most important and productive thing you do in a day. The days when you simply can't get started tend to follow a pattern—usually they occur when your brain has decided that you need relaxation or, more likely, sleep.

Keep in mind, though, that too much break time often invites wandering and meandering before finally returning to what you needed to get done in the first place. Besides, most people don't fastidiously ensure that their breaks last only as long as planned. Could that be you?

When it comes to starting a task or project, people tend to procrastinate if they lack either a clear starting point or a logical sequence of steps to take. Projects are successfully executed by those individuals who craft a succinct outline or plan of attack and have the energy and discipline to stick to it. (Sounds good except for that "energy and discipline" part, huh?)

Action-oriented role models are all around you. By and large, they are the winners in life. (This could have you unfortunately inching closer to the loser category.) While you previously may not have considered the value of studying the behaviors of action-takers and high achievers, now is the time to do so.

Sometimes the only way to get started on a task is to dive into it headlong, cold turkey, and not allow yourself the opportunity to stray. Watch out if you start believing that you alone are the only one who can handle all tasks! You are not omnipotent and are never likely to be.

If you find yourself continually switching between projects, you may be playing a subtle game of procrastination wherein you're actually avoiding the one key task among the many that need to be finished. When you have been putting off something to the point that you are appalling yourself, perhaps it is time to seek help from others!

Routine deadlines convey benefits. When you're able to relate your responsibilities to the larger question of how it contributes to your team, division, department, organization, or society in general, it's much easier to stay on track. Even non-routine, drastic, one-of-a-kind deadlines often convey benefits to those who are astute enough to comprehend and work toward meeting them. Young or old, the more things that compete for your time and attention, the more even small tasks will loom over you. Everyone today feels the enormity of what they need to get done. Yet, many of the items that you face require only a few minutes each. It's not that bad.

The fears that accompany certain situations you face need not be debilitating. If you allow yourself to feel the fear of whatever task you have been putting off, you actually position yourself to begin the task at hand with greater ease.

If you find yourself reluctant to handle or even begin a task that needs to be done, employ language such as "I choose," "I want," "I will," and "I will be happy to," or at least, "I guess I will." If it's your thing, practice in front of the mirror—though, I wouldn't suggest doing this in a restaurant bathroom. If you're straightforward with yourself and acknowledge when you are procrastinating, you're that much closer to taking action. Even the smallest action in pursuit of a long-term goal is far better than nothing.

If you have trouble getting started on something, review evaluations and letters of praise you may have received from within your organization as well as those from external sources. Even birthday cards from grandma count here. Assuming she likes you, that is.

Reframe tasks, however seemingly mundane, as something contributing to your long-term prosperity, growth, career advancement, or domestic tranquility, and you'll be far more productive. It might make clearing the leaves from the gutter or delousing the cat have a higher meaning. People often avoid routine filing because they don't see the connection between filing and its future impact on their careers and lives. Simply organizing materials often represents a good, pre-emptive move in the battle against procrastination. If you can find the right file, you shoot down one more lame excuse for not working on it.

People have a tendency not to get started on a specific project if they know there are going to be interruptions or bottlenecks. If you take care of contingencies, you have a far greater chance of starting and staying with the project from the outset. Often it makes sense to handle minor tasks before tackling something larger. When you only have one project or task at hand, your odds of maintaining clarity and focus increase dramatically. When you have no tasks, procrastination is no longer your primary problem.

It is also important to create an environment in which you can work at your best. Sometimes people will procrastinate on a project if they fear being interrupted. To eliminate this possibility, remove distractions—whatever or whomever they may be. Implement your zone scenario, as in "zone in," not "zone out"—you will greatly increase your probability of achieving results on the task at hand.

Sometimes tasks are simply too challenging—you can't face them alone. There, I've said it. So, affiliate—seek to work with people who are facing a similar challenge. If you find yourself procrastinating when it comes to getting started on a project, then find a knowledgeable, trusted trail guide who can jump-start your motivation and recharge your enthusiasm. For long-term success, seek out a viable partner who can help you get started and stay on course.

If you have to tackle something on Monday, briefly view the project on Friday before you go home for the weekend. That way you'll have some familiarity with the particulars come Monday—you'll be in a better position to estimate how much time to allot for the project and you'll cut your stress load by half. This is a case where familiarity does *not* breed contempt.

Carefully select three to five major activities in support of some task you want to accomplish and then devise and sign a contract with yourself that aids you in completing that task. Making deeply pronounced choices, such as "I choose to easily get started on the task at hand," is an effective way to overcome procrastination.

It's a well-known fact that positively reinforced behavior tends to be repeated. If you're facing an unpleasant task, follow it up with something you enjoy doing. When you have control over the order in which you tackle steps on the way to achieving a task, attempt to handle the seemingly unpleasant elements first. Find some element of your task that you can complete quickly and easily, and score an immediate "win." Then look high and low for other scores.

If you're having a hard time getting started on a task, promise yourself that you'll engage in it for only four minutes. Record your explanation of why you can't get started—the hardship of actually doing something about your project is often more palatable than the hardship of having to listen to your own worn-out, feeble excuses. Another technique that works: When you've been postponing a project, write your quest on several Post-it pads and place them throughout your "world."

Also, when you engage in any task, work beyond the halfway point before taking a "midway" pause or switching to something else. By taking care of the "heavy half" first, and acknowledging this completion, you leave yourself far more energized to complete the shorter, lighter second half.

To ensure that you complete more of what you want or need to accomplish, you need to safeguard, nurture, and support your propensity to stay on a (proverbial) roll. From the standpoint of effectively starting on a task or project, multitasking is not the world's best idea. You want to give your full and undivided attention to the task at hand.

Another useful exercise is the following: Write the sentence, "I have now come to the end of my life and I'm disappointed that I didn't _____." Do this exercise ten times. Don't think too hard about it. Just write down what readily comes to mind. How did you finish that sentence? Whatever you came up with first is probably something you want to do right away. Stuff that comes up later, you can skip for now. A key thing to remember about procrastination is not to be overwhelmed by the tyranny of the urgent—know what is important.

Afterword

In *The Fountain of Age*, Betty Friedan closes with a remarkable paragraph:

> *I am myself at this age. It took me these years to put the missing pieces together, to confront my own age in terms of integrity and generativity, moving into the unknown future with a comfort now, instead of being stuck in the past. I have never felt so free.*

So, what kind of projects can you tackle to improve your life? What kind of plans do you want to make, given the fact that today represents a new opportunity to reclaim your life? The following is a set of new ideas you might want to entertain. These aren't ones that traditionally make achievers' lists, but they can be important to the quality and possibly quantity of your life.

1. *Weight.* What weight do you want to be one year from now or five years from now? What size waistline do you want to have? Probably something a wee bit smaller than you have now. Do you want to become as fit as you've been in the past? It's possible, but it's a choice you'll have to make first.
2. *Blood pressure.* I'll bet you never thought of this. Would you like to get your blood pressure down to 120 over 80? What foods and habits are you willing to give up to keep your blood pressure at a safe, healthy level? If you eat like a bird, you live as long as an elephant.

3. *Resting pulse per minute.* How hard is your heart working for you right now? Is your resting pulse above 80? Actually, 70 beats per minute, and even 60, is quite possible.

4. *Hours of sleep nightly.* One year or five years from now, how much do you want to be sleeping—actually sleeping, not just tossing and turning in bed—medication free? It's up to you.

5. *Healthy foods regularly consumed.* You may not be able to eat the recommended three to five servings of vegetables each day, or the two to three servings of fruit, but you could probably add a lot more of both to your diet. (Fruit Roll-Ups and veggie dip do not count.) You don't have to visit a health food store to eat healthfully. You need only choose fresh foods from your regular supermarket.

> *"His resolve is not to seem, but to be, the best."*
> —AESCHYLUS

6. *Vitamins taken regularly.* If you're over thirty, this grows in importance each day. Do you take a multivitamin? Do you take specific vitamins throughout the day to ensure peak performance? When is the last time you visited a nutritionist or dietitian and figured out which supplements would be best given your lifestyle and physiology? Okay . . . then when will be the first time?

7. *Great novels read.* Which great novels would you like to read, but year after year do not begin? If you want to improve the quality of your life for the rest of your life, you can start with the next book you read. So put down that romance novel. Toss Fabio to the side. Believe me, it'll feel good.

8. *Classic or inspiring movies viewed.* Sure, it's easy enough to rent the latest shoot 'em up or action thriller. Instead, what about

a good biographical video? Or how about a historical novel on video? What about a documentary? Don't laugh; some of them are more entertaining and certainly more redeeming than the average flick. At any given moment, you have a lot of alternatives in terms of what you're viewing.

9. *Family involvement.* Maybe you're already adept here, but perhaps it's an area to revisit. Have you been to one of your son's clarinet lessons? Have you ever watched your daughter for a full soccer practice? Have you had a real family outing—not the kind where you go to a theme park, spend money, and have hectic fun, but where you bring a picnic basket, hike together, talk to each other, and spend the day in a quiet and enjoyable setting?

It could be one of the best days of your life.

Further Reading

Assagioli, Roberto. *The Act of Will.* New York: Viking Press, 1973.

Ayan, Jordan. *Aha! 10 Ways to Free Your Creative Spirit and Find Your Great Ideas.* New York: Crown, 1997.

Blakeslee, Thomas. *Beyond the Conscious Mind.* New York: Plenum Press, 1996.

Bliss, Edwin C. *Doing It Now: A Twelve-Step Program for Curing Procrastination and Achieving Your Goals.* New York: Scribner, 1983.

Breininger, Dorothy, and Debby S. Bitticks. *Time Efficiency Makeover: Own Your Time and Your Life by Conquering Procrastination.* Deerfield Beach, FL: HCI, 2005.

Burka, Jane, and Lenora M. Wuen. *Procrastination: Why You Do It, What to Do About It.* 3rd Ed. Reading, MA: Addison-Wesley, 2004.

Cameron, Julia. *The Artist's Way.* Los Angeles: Jeremy P. Tarcher/Perigee, 1992.

Caroselli, Marlene. *Defeating Procrastination: 52 Fail-Safe Tips for Keeping Time on Your Side.* Mission, KS: SkillPath, 1997.

Cathcart, Jim. *The Acorn Principle.* New York: St. Martin's, 1998.

Conwell, Russell H. *Acres of Diamonds.* New York: Jove, 1995.

Csikszentmihalyi, Mihaly. *Flow: The Psychology of Optimal Experience.* New York: Harper & Row, 1990.

Daniels, Aubrey. *Bringing Out the Best in People.* New York: McGraw-Hill, 2000.

Davidson, Jeff. *Breathing Space: Living & Working at a Comfortable Pace in a Sped-up Society.* Charleston, S.C.: Booksurge, 2007.

―――. *The Complete Idiot's Guide to Reaching Your Goals.* New York: Alpha Books, 1998.

Dawson, Roger. *The 13 Secrets of Power Performance.* Englewood Cliffs, NJ: Prentice-Hall, 1994.

Douglas, Mack R. *How to Make a Habit of Succeeding.* Grand Rapids, MI: Zondervan, 1972.

Drucker, Peter F. *The Effective Executive.* New York: Harper & Row, 1967.

Dyer, Wayne W. *How to Be a No Limit Person.* New York: Berkley, 1980.

Emmett, Rita. *The Procrastinator's Handbook.* New York: Walker, 2000.

Everett, Henry C. *How to Reach Your Goals: How to Conquer Procrastination, Fear, and Other Obstacles on Your Way.* Lincoln, NE: IUniverse.com, 2000.

Fiore, Neil. *The Now Habit: A Strategic Program for Overcoming Procrastination and Enjoying Guilt-Free Play.* New York: Tarcher, 2007.

Freeman, Dave, Neil Teplica, and the editors of WhatsGoingOn .com with Jennifer Coonce. *100 Things to Do Before You Die: Travel Events You Just Can't Miss.* Dallas, TX: Taylor Publishing, 1999.

Friedan, Betty. *The Fountain of Age.* New York: Simon & Schuster, 1993.

Fritz, Robert. *The Path of Least Resistance.* New York: Fawcett, 1989.

Fulghum, Robert. *All I Really Need to Know I Learned in Kindergarten.* New York: Fawcett, 1993.

Goleman, Daniel. *Emotional Intelligence*. New York: Bantam, 1995.

Helmstetter, Shad. *What to Say When You Talk to Yourself*. New York: Pocket Books, 1990.

Horney, Karen. *Neurosis and Human Growth*. New York: Norton, 1991.

Jeffers, Susan. *Feel the Fear and Do It Anyway*. New York: Fawcett Books, 1992.

Jolley, Willie. *A Setback Is a Setup for a Comeback*. New York: St. Martin's, 1999.

Knaus, William J. *Do It Now! Break the Procrastination Habit*. New York: J. Wiley, 1998.

———. *Do It Now: How To Stop Procrastinating*. Englewood Cliffs, NJ: Prentice-Hall, 1979.

Koenig, Larry J. *Getting Things Done Now: 17 Proven Principles For Overcoming Procrastination*. Nashville, TN: Thomas Nelson Publishers, 2006.

Lakein, Alan. *How to Get Control of Your Time and Your Life*. New York: P.H. Wyden, 1973.

Lively, Lynn. *The Procrastinator's Guide to Success*. New York: McGraw-Hill, 1999.

Maltz, Maxwell. *Psycho-cybernetics*. New York: Pocket Books, 1989.

Pagonis, William G., with Jeffrey L. Cruikshank. *Moving Mountains*. Boston: Harvard Business School Press, 1992.

Porat, Frieda. *Creative Procrastination: Organizing Your Own Life*. San Francisco: Harper & Row, 1980.

Roberts, M. Susan. *Living Without Procrastination: How to Stop Postponing Your Life*. Oakland, CA: New Harbinger, 1995.

Salsbury, Glenna. *The Art of the Fresh Start*. Deerfield Beach, FL: Health Communications, 1995.

Sapadin, Linda, and Jack Maguire. *It's About Time! The Six Styles of Procrastination and How to Overcome Them.* New York: Penguin, 1997.

Sugarman, Joseph. *Success Forces.* Chicago: Contemporary Books, 1980.

Tracy, Brian. *Eat That Frog! 21 Great Ways to Stop Procrastinating and Get More Done in Less Time.* San Francisco: Berrett-Koehler, 2007.

Tullier, L. Michelle. *The Complete Idiot's Guide to Overcoming Procrastination.* Indianapolis: Alpha Books, 1999.

Viscott, David S. *Emotional Resilience.* New York: Crown, 1997.

Watson, Donna. *101 Simple Ways to Be Good to Yourself: How to Discover Peace and Joy in Your Life.* New York: Bard, 1992.

Glossary

accommodate: to tolerate the situation as the only alternative.

administrivia: small, often unimportant stuff you tend to use to avoid big, important stuff.

antsy: to be agitated or overly excited.

aromatherapy: use of essential oils and herbs to treat specific health- and stress-related conditions.

assimilation: the process of adapting a new idea to a process already in progress.

atmosphere: in a business context, how an environment appeals to consumers.

axiom: a truism of life; a premise that people accept as valid.

balance: to bring into proportion or harmony; to be in equilibrium.

completion: closure.

compromise: a settlement in which both sides make concessions, or a solution that is midway between two alternatives.

contingency plan: a backup course of action to be initiated in the event that the original course of action encounters significant barriers.

day units: a way to measure time toward a goal—you can count six hours of steady work as a day, for example.

dynamic bargain: an agreement you make with yourself to assess what you've accomplished (and what more you want to accomplish) from time to time throughout the day, adjusting to new conditions as they emerge.

elucidate: to clearly explain something.

empower: to commission to take action on one's own.

equilibrium: the state in which driving forces and restraining forces are roughly equal.

ergonomics: the science that examines how devices should most smoothly accommodate the human body and human activity.

escrow: a fund held in reserve.

germination: development, growth, or maturation.

goal statement: an objective or desired result that is written down, measurable, and has a specific time frame.

homeostasis: the state of balance and harmonious function characterizing all healthy, living organisms.

hone: to sharpen or file to a fine edge.

hydration: when your body's tissues are sufficiently filled with water. To be dehydrated is to be parched.

impetus: momentum.

learning anxiety: a restraining force that most of us feel to some degree when we're compelled to learn something new, and which opposes both learning and change.

leisure: enjoying rewarding activities free from work and preoccupation with work.

limiting language: *shoulds*, *oughts*, or *musts* that negatively affect your opinion about a task, especially about starting it.

meditation: quieting the conscious mind and enabling it to roam freely without intentional direction.

meditative: a contemplative state, in which one is immersed in deep reflection.

mentor: a wise adviser, teacher, or coach.

motivation: inspiration or drive, from the Latin word for "to move."

networking: developing personal contacts for exchange of information to further one's career.

nuance: a slight hint or subtle aspect of something.

objectivity: a clear, impartial, and neutral focus.

palatable: the quality of being agreeable, enjoyable, or tasty.

paradox: a situation in which two seemingly independent items or events exist at the same time or in the same place.

perfectionism: the practice of attempting to make things perfect; often a disguise for not proceeding or for being discontent.

piddling: something that is paltry, trivial, or inconsequential.

priority: that which is most important to you.

proverbial: alleged or fictional, as opposed to real and tangible.

rationalize: to justify or mentally minimize the negative aspects of a situation.

reflection: deliberation or thoughtfulness.

reframe: to think of a task in a new context or from a different perspective.

reinvention: noteworthy movement from point A in your life to point B.

rekindle: in the context of a relationship: to renew or to reunite; generally, to reinvest your time and energy.

role model: a person who, as a result of position, expertise, actions and/or personality, serves as an example of good, productive, or effective conduct.

sanctity: the holiness, virtue, or worthiness of a person, place, or thing.

seed work: tasks you can easily assign to someone else because the downside risk if he or she botches the task is negligible.

self-talk: the often subconscious, internal comments that people make about their own abilities, capacities, or inclinations.

semantic: of or relating to words or word choices.

sound screen: an electronic device that creates a sound "barrier," which masks or mutes the effects of sounds emanating from beyond the barrier.

status quo: the existing state of affairs, or how conditions are traditionally expected to be.

synergy: when one plus one equals more than two; it's when the end result equals more than the sum of the parts.

time-shifting: a method of taking care of tasks in a different order than was planned; a form of creative procrastination.

triage: the practice of quickly examining a variety of items and allocating them based on what needs to be handled immediately, what can be handled later, and what can be ignored altogether.

venue: a setting, place, or locale.

visualization: forming a mental image to foster a sense of calm and a more ready focus on tasks.

white noise: a noninvasive, nondisruptive sound, like that of rushing water, a fan, or a distant motor, or a constant background noise that drowns out other noises.

yoga: yoga means "union," referring to the union of the mind and the body.

zone: the circumstances under which you do your best, most productive work.

About the Author

JEFF DAVIDSON is self-starter par excellence. Still, being all too human, he procrastinates as much as anybody on the planet (Earth that is). He has learned the importance of having a variety of techniques at his disposal to blast through procrastination, thereby limiting its debilitating effects and allowing him to proceed with the task or project at hand.

Jeff is known as an author and professional who offers new perspectives and fresh solutions to the career and life balance problems that people face today. Jeff's speeches have been featured in *Vital Speeches of the Day* on eight occasions, along with those of Dr. Henry Kissinger, Lee Iacocca, George Bush (senior), William Bennett, Michael Eisner, Jimmy Carter, Alan Greenspan, and the Dalai Lama. Some crowd. He has shared the spotlight on covers of magazines with Tony Robbins and Dr. Wayne Dyer.

He has been featured in seventy-two of the top seventy-five newspapers in America, based on circulation, including *USA Today*, the *Washington Post*, the *New York Times*, the *Los Angeles Times*, and the *Chicago Tribune,* but the *Wall Street Journal* eludes him. A five-time state winner of the U.S. Small Business Administration's Media Advocate of the Year Award, Jeff has published more than 3,550 articles on the topics of life-balance, management and marketing effectiveness, and time management in nearly every type of magazine, journal, newsletter, and 'zine imaginable.

Jeff has attracted clients such as America Online, Lufthansa, Wells Fargo, NationsBank, IBM, Swissotel, Executone, American Express, Westinghouse, Uncle Joe's Eat and Run, and more than

500 other leading organizations and associations including the U.S. Treasury, National Association of Realtors, Club Managers Association of America, and the American Congress of Healthcare Executives. He is a columnist in three publications, an audio columnist on Selling Power Live, and a frequent Webinar presenter for the Manage Smarter, Audio Educators, and Apex Performance Systems.

Through his popular books such *The Joy of Simple Living, The Complete Guide to Public Speaking, Breathing Space,* and *The Complete Idiot's Guide to Time Management* as well as other titles in that series, Jeff has averaged 100,000 books sold annually for five years running in the highly competitive field of self-help, business, and how-to books. Love those book buyers! His earlier version of this book, *The 60 Second Procrastinator,* as well as his companion book, *The 60 Second Organizer,* have been published in Arabic, Indonesian, Italian, Spanish, Japanese, Korean, and Turkish, and in English for India, Singapore, and Malaysia.

Jeff can be reached via e-mail at *Jeff@BreathingSpace.com* and found on the Web at *www.BreathingSpace.com*, which offers information on his keynote speeches and seminars, including *No Time, No Clarity? No Problem!*™, *Managing the Pace with Grace*®, *Choosing When it's Confusing*®, and *Managing Information and Communication Overload*®.